Praise for *Looking for God in Messy Places*

"This is beautiful and brilliant stuff, profound and plain, incredibly human, wise and charming. I trusted and enjoyed every word."

—**Anne Lamott**, *New York Times* best-selling author

"For any who feel frustrated and world-weary, and who want more than just wishful thinking or superficial spirituality, this book is for you! In these pages, my friend Jake Owensby poignantly shows how LOVE is what can truly give us hope to carry on: real love, God's love for us, our love for each other, right here, right now, in all the struggles of this messy life. And God knows, we need this book NOW!"

—**Bishop Michael Curry**, Presiding Bishop of The Episcopal Church and author of *Love is the Way: Holding on to Hope in Troubling Times*

"Jake Owensby doesn't hide from the messiness of life. He invites us to live with our eyes wide open, finding God in beauty and pain, wonder and sorrow, clarity and mystery. This is a book to heal broken hearts and restore weary souls."

—**Brian D. McLaren**, author of *Faith After Doubt*

"For any of us who has struggled to hope in these dark days, Jake Owensby illuminates the most important theological truth I know: If God is truly a God who loves, then help is always on the way, and hope is never in vain."

—**Greg Garrett**, author of *A Long, Long Way: Hollywood's Unfinished Journey from Racism to Redemption*, and (with Rowan Williams) *In Conversation: Rowan Williams and Greg Garrett*

"I read a lot of books that leave me feeling smarter, funnier, or more entertained. When I put down Jake Owensby's *Looking for God in Messy Places*, I had grown wiser. In these times when we could easily despair, Owensby digs deep into his life and the human experience in order to unearth a solid hope, rooted and grounded in faith."

—**Rev. Carol Howard Merritt**, Senior Pastor of ̶ ̶ Church and author of *Healing ̶ ̶*

Looking for God in Messy Places

Looking for GOD in Messy Places

A Book about Hope

How to find it. Practice it. Grow in it.

JAKE OWENSBY

Abingdon Press | Nashville

LOOKING FOR GOD IN MESSY PLACES
A BOOK ABOUT HOPE: HOW TO FIND IT. PRACTICE IT. GROW IN IT.

Library of Congress Control Number: 2020950680

ISBN 13: 978-1-7910-1322-6

21 22 23 24 25 26 27 28 29 30—10 9 8 7 6 5 4 3 2 1
MANUFACTURED IN THE UNITED STATES OF AMERICA

For Addi and Bennett
Love, love, love

Love and goodness ... are the reasons we have hope.

—Anne Lamott,
Almost Everything: Notes on Hope

*Do not depend on the hope of results.... You may have to face
the fact that your work will be apparently worthless and even
achieve no result at all, if not perhaps results opposite to what
you expect. As you get used to this idea you start more and more
to concentrate not on the results but on the value, the rightness,
the truth of the work itself.*

—Thomas Merton,
The Hidden Ground of Love: Letters by Thomas Merton

CONTENTS

CONTENTS

FOREWORD

I want to introduce you to a friend of mine, Bishop Jake Owensby. Several years ago he invited me to teach the clergy in the region of Louisiana where he serves. After the event, he invited me to join him on a drive around the diocese. Usually when hosts take me on such tours, the itinerary includes historical sites, lively downtowns, elegant church buildings, and streets of nice houses with tidy gardens. People like showing their best to guests. I've seen much of America this way.

Jake, however, bypassed the typical venues. Instead, he showed me a closed rural hospital, neighborhoods of shotgun houses, struggling farms, and small churches. Along the way, he told me stories of bad government, purposeful neglect of the poor, racial tensions, and political division. He also shared stories about some of the people he'd come to know, revealing how much faith and joy could be found in the Louisiana countryside. And he talked about his mother who, as a teenager, had been held in a Nazi prison camp.

On that drive, I also learned that Bishop Jake was a philosopher, a former college professor. I laughed inwardly, because I can't say that I'm entirely comfortable with either bishops or philosophers. Perhaps it is just my experience, but I've often found bishops distant and philosophers preoccupied, more interested in the machinations of arcane institutions or intellectual conventions than in the messiness of everyday life. However, in the driving tour around rural Louisiana, I forgot about Jake's titles and roles.

Instead, I found myself trusting the most gracious and thoughtful of guides, a person who was taking me through the landscape of his heart.

That landscape was inhabited by people who lived on the margins—poor Southern folks often ignored by middle-class church, both white and black; alcoholics and the barely recovered; immigrants hidden from view; abused and impoverished single mothers. To him, all these people are the body of Christ, whether they are members of his church or not, the body he has been called to serve. And, above all, God inhabits every place—the woods and marshes, the sky and the storms. There, in western Louisiana, a geography overlooked or held in derision by more elite Americans, Jake finds hope. Authentic hope. I had never imagined Louisiana as a holy place until that day—until that drive. By the time he dropped me off at the airport, I had both seen his world through the eyes of faith and made a new friend.

I wish Jake could drive you through his Louisiana diocese, but this book is the next best option. In *Looking for God in Messy Places*, he will take you through the working-class American South to Nazi Germany and all manner of everyday places, where hope arises in the most unlikely and despairing circumstances. And although he writes of faith and philosophical ideas, his itinerary is neither churchy nor academic. Instead, he invites you to join him on a journey through the landscape of God. By the time you wend through these pages, you will see what he sees—the world nested with love, the very nidus of hope. And, trust me, you will have made a new friend.

—Diana Butler Bass

INTRODUCTION

*If love is greater than hope, as Paul says it is, this may be true in
part because love is prior to hope, a condition of it.*
—Marilynne Robinson, *What Are We Doing Here? Essays*

These days Anne Lamott may be an accomplished skier, but a few years
ago she would warm up with the beginners for a while and then stick with
the easiest intermediate slope. Once, after several goes on her usual course,
she hopped on the chairlift for yet another run and grew momentarily
confused. The jump-off looked unfamiliar, and before she realized that it
was indeed the correct one, Anne found herself five or so feet above the
ground, heading toward a more difficult trail. She dove from the moving
chair. Not with a confident, James Bond–like leap. It was more of a tumble
that ended with a crash landing. Most of her fellow skiers pretended not to
have seen what happened. She waved off the few sympathetic witnesses who
offered to help, acting as if this is just the sort of quirky thing she does. And
then the nausea hit. On the verge of passing out, she asked Jesus for help.
She writes,

> I don't know how long I stood there with my hand clamped to
> my mouth, only my poles and a frayed, consignment-store faith
> to support me. All I knew was that help is always on the way,
> a hundred percent of the time. . . . I know that when I call out,

God will be near, and hear, and help eventually. Of course, it is
the "eventually" that throws one into despair.[1]

This is a book for those of us who are feeling the weight of that
"eventually." For those whose struggles have been long and for those who
are growing weary from heavy burdens. For those facing an unforeseen crisis
or for those enduring a slow personal train wreck. For those whose throats
have grown raw from crying for justice and for those whose wounds have
gone unhealed. This is a book about hope, and I have written it especially for
those who refuse to yield to discouragement and despair.

I follow Jesus, so anything I say about hope ends up pointing in his
direction in some unexpected ways. So let me admit from the start that
many of the typical reasons Christians give for having hope don't work
for me—something we will be exploring throughout this book. Some of
us derive our hope from the doctrines of the Resurrection and the Second
Coming. In the next life, we will be free from the sorrow, pain, and strife of
this one. We will be reunited with those we love and reconciled to everyone.
God will set all things right. The wolf will lie down with the lamb. There
will be perfect justice and perpetual peace. I believe in life after life—in
the resurrection of the body, and I believe that God is at work restoring the
entire creation to a wholeness that exceeds even my wildest imaginings. Yet,
my assent to these doctrines is not what gives me hope.

Hope is something more, something deeper and more abiding.
Hope is what keeps us going when the odds just don't seem to be in our
favor. The setbacks are piling up, but still we get out of bed morning after
morning. That's hope. We keep swimming even though the tide is against
us. Hope tells us, "It's worth it." Doctrines don't do this, at least not for me.
But God does, and I don't mean my *idea* of God. I mean my awareness of
God at work in all the messy places of my life, my awareness of God raising
me to a new life through forgiveness and self-acceptance, my awareness of
God mending relationships, changing hearts, and healing wounds. This
is God's love made real in the particulars of my life. My experience of the

relentless power of God's love in these ways gives me the sense that this life—the one I am actually living in all its sweetness and frustration, joy and pain—is worth living.

Hope is knowing in your gut, in the center of your being, that your life is worth living even when you have grown bone weary with struggle, sorrow, anxiety, and grief. You have felt the weight of that "eventually" while waiting on God's promises. You have had what I call an "Ecclesiastes Moment."

The author of Ecclesiastes wrote, "I considered all that my hands had done and the toil I had spent in doing it, and again, all was vanity and a chasing after wind" (Ecclesiastes 2:11). In other words, life is pointless. A chasing after wind. We all wind up in the same place: six feet under. This is what I mean by an Ecclesiastes Moment: being drawn up short by the soul-numbing thought that maybe all your sweat, tender devotion, giddy joy, and costly sacrifice amount in the end to nothing.

Some might respond quickly to this by saying, "This life is all about getting into heaven in the next life. What happens here on planet Earth is not supposed to give you hope. Of course we die. But if you believe in Jesus, you'll go to heaven." While I, too, put my trust in the resurrection, I do not think that anticipating a continued existence in the hereafter makes my life worth living *now*. For that matter, I think that such an understanding of eternal life is not found in the Scriptures.

Though the point of the resurrection is often considered to be getting into the Good Place, where we will enjoy doing fun things and being with beloved people forever, Scripture teaches us that the resurrection is about being transformed by an intimate union with God. To use Paul's language, our relationship with God in Christ makes us a "new creation" (2 Corinthians 5:17). While our relationship with Christ stretches beyond the grave into eternity, it begins in all the ordinary days, embarrassing spectacles, tight spots, dark corners, and tender moments that are our life on planet Earth. Dying and rising—growing from a bundle of divinely-given potential, toxic family hangovers, and ill-fitting cultural hand-me-downs toward our true self—takes place right now in Christ. Our hope does not rest on the anticipation of the next life. Instead, our assurance that this life is worth living comes from noticing that God keeps showing up in the midst of it. Responding to God's loving presence in the here and now stretches us toward the persons we are meant to be. Being loved and giving love empower us to endure hardship, to overcome adversity, and to resist injustice.

My central premise in this book is that hope comes from our awareness of God's love for us and our response to that love as we extend it to each other in the present, especially in life's chaotic, puzzling, exhausting, and heartrending places. God is present even when we feel shattered or soul-weary. When we struggle to carry on or feel insignificant. When we are overwhelmed by our ordinary busyness or frozen in place by loss or regret. Throughout these pages, I am responding to a raw, honest question: How do we carry on when we realize that this existence is so fragile that it will be broken again and again and that it moves toward death with each breath? This is the question lurking in our Ecclesiastes Moments. We need a "why" to keep going. And the abysmal truth is that this "why" is never merely a given. We have to choose it, or assent to it, or be chosen by it. Hope is how we inhabit this world with a vital "why." We trust in our marrow that this beautiful, horrifying, joyful, heartrending life is worth living as it actually is.

My first lessons in hope came from my mother, and for years I completely misunderstood them. When life got hard, Mom would say, "Tomorrow is another day." She said it when other kids bullied me at school because of my speech impediment, when we were broke and on the run from her abusive husband, and when we were living in a car and begging for food. I assumed that she meant that tomorrow—or some other future date—would bring a happy ending. Things would eventually look up. Our circumstances might be lousy right now, but what we were going through would lead us to a better place. Once we got there, all our struggles would have been worthwhile. This sounded like baseless, wishful thinking to me. I could not have been more mistaken.

My mother learned about hope in a place designed to drive people to despair. At the age of fifteen, she entered Mauthausen-Gusen Concentration Camp, and hope was the key to her survival in the face of the systematic brutality, humiliation, and deprivation of that place. Hope did not protect her from starvation, disease, torture, or execution. Hope is what kept her going each day.

As far as my mother could tell, prisoners left that camp only as corpses. There was no reliable news of an approaching Allied army. Everybody worked long, arduous hours on a diet of five hundred calories a day. People frequently collapsed from hunger, exhaustion, and disease. Each succeeding sunrise brought greater misery. Wishful thinking of escape or liberation was extinguished in Mauthausen.

It wasn't until I visited the camp and stood on those grounds myself that it finally dawned on me what Mom was getting at by telling me that tomorrow is another day. She had meant something like this: "Today is the day that you've been given. This is the life you have. And that life is worth living. Keep going. Don't give up. Do the good that you can here and now." She wasn't much of a Bible reader, but I think she was echoing Jesus: "Do not worry about tomorrow, for tomorrow will bring worries of its own. Today's trouble is enough for today" (Matthew 6:34).

Yes, I believe hope is knowing in your gut, in your very bones, that this life is worth living. To be hopeful is to have a "why" that enables you not merely to endure all manner of hardship and suffering, heartache and disappointment, but to resist, to overcome, and even to thrive. Hope is not a head thing. It is a heart thing. My mother had her own Ecclesiastes Moment, and she learned to draw hope from within the present because that is where God showed up. I believe that is where God shows up for us, too.

You can profess the Christian faith without having an Ecclesiastes Moment that leads to an encounter with the felt presence of God—an encounter that leaves you breathless, turns you upside down, or makes you weep with joy or laugh like a toddler. But that kind of faith, which is grounded on religious principle and doctrine alone, is a social order rather than a soul-stretching, life-shaping friendship with the risen Christ.

On the night before Roman authorities murdered him on the cross, Jesus explicitly told his friends that he would not abandon them. His teachings about the Holy Spirit say, in essence, that God is perpetually in, around, and between us. God is right here. Right now. Always. Reaching out to be an essential part of our lives (John 14:18; 15:5-7). The problem is that we struggle to be aware of God's presence. As Christian Wiman puts it, "We can't perceive, and we miss the God who misses—as in longs for—us."[2]

The spiritual challenge, then, is to become aware of God's presence— especially in messy places—with such vulnerability, humility, and yearning that God's love for us transforms who we are. That love shapes our habitual way of being in this world into the way of love: Love of God. Love of neighbor. Love that makes life worth living. Love that leads us to hope.

That is the journey we will be taking together in this book—a journey of learning to look for God in the here and now. Because genuine hope begins and ends with the God who shows up in all our messy, beautiful, ordinary, and soul-wrenching places.

PART I

How Love Gives Us Hope

The very least you can do in your life is to figure out what you hope for. And the most you can do is live inside that hope. Not admire it from a distance but live right in it, under its roof.

—Barbara Kingsolver, *Animal Dreams*

1

A LIFE WORTH LIVING

I am a frayed and nibbled survivor in a fallen world,
and I am getting along.

—Annie Dillard, *Pilgrim at Tinker Creek*

Joy and I had been stunned to learn that our daughter, Meredith, had a hole in her heart. She was an energetic, happy baby. During a routine healthy-baby visit, our pediatrician had heard what might be a murmur. He told us that it was probably nothing. Her development was very robust. But to be safe, he referred us to a specialist. Believing that the visit would be nothing more than a formality, Joy took Meredith to the specialist alone, and I went to work as usual. I will never forget the sound of Joy's voice when she called from our church's office following the visit to the cardiologist. Fighting back tears, she told me that Meredith was facing open-heart surgery.

Plenty of people sought to comfort and reassure us with prayers, kind words, and casseroles. I remained calm and told everyone, including Joy, that I was confident in a positive outcome. God would get us all through this ordeal. Meredith was going to be fine. We simply had to keep the faith and remain fervent in prayer. God wouldn't let us down. Even as I said these things, I knew that I was a big, fat phony. From the moment we got the news about Meredith's heart through the days and weeks leading up to the

3

surgery, Joy and I nearly suffocated with dread. Time crawled. Each routine task took immense effort. Joy lost a startling amount of weight. I quickly found every ounce she had shed. When Joy is worried, she cannot eat. By contrast, anxiousness drives me to scarf down everything in sight, and I was doing nothing to soothe my troubled heart. Instead, over and over, my imagination leapt to worst-case scenarios. Images of the surgeon cracking Meredith's little sternum would come uninvited into my mind's eye. My blood pressure would spike, my mouth would go dry, and I would feel my heart pounding in my chest. I feared that she wouldn't make it off the table. Sure, my lips were saying all sorts of pious-sounding things. But just under the skin I was a terrified mess.

You might be thinking that I put up a strong front because I had learned that showing emotion makes you look weak. I confess that I grew up in the John Wayne/Clint Eastwood era, and my father wanted me to be a stoic man's man. But honestly, I was a miserable disappointment to him. According to the Meyers-Briggs Type Inventory, I'm an NF: an intuitive-feeler. Oh sure, I've got grit. I'm no quitter or shrinking violet. But, man, my feelings make themselves known, and I can't help but intuit the emotional temperature of any room I enter. So, no, I wasn't suffering from low emotional intelligence. Believe it or not, I was sincerely trying to be hopeful. Because, well, that's what people of faith do. Right?

The apostle Paul said that faith, hope, and love are the foundations of the Christian life (1 Corinthians 13:13). So, the thinking often goes that if you're a person of faith, you're supposed to be certain that God will work things out for you. We learn that's what it means to hope. People often express the idea to me, that, "You have to trust that God has a plan. Everything happens for a reason. Everybody faces challenges and disappointments, but God makes even the hardest life worth living. That's because God uses everything that happens in life to bring you to a better place, a place of true happiness. (Well, at least God does this for those who keep the faith.) So, if you want God to grant you your heart's desire, you need to push your doubts aside."

I was ashamed to admit that I was struggling with this popular understanding of hope. I kept trying to force myself to believe that God was in complete control and that my faith would somehow result in a successful surgery and a complete recovery, but I never genuinely embraced that sort of hope. To be perfectly honest, I don't even call that spiritual posture hope anymore. It's more accurately described as wishful thinking. In wishful thinking, the prospect of getting what we want—a healed daughter, a soul mate, eternal bliss in paradise—is what keeps us going in this world. God serves merely as the guarantor that we will eventually get our heart's desire. But leveraging God to give us the outcome we desire is not hope. Being hopeful is the sense that this life—no matter how untidy or harrowing—is inherently worth living.

Don't get me wrong. Our relationship with God is the *source* of hope. That's because God is with us and for us in this world. We live this life to the fullest by loving. And when we love, we encounter the God who loves us. Hope is how we lean into this world as God's beloved children. It is what keeps us going, no matter what. But it's far more than wishful thinking.

Beyond Wishful Thinking

There is nothing wrong with looking for favorable outcomes or working to improve your circumstances. Anticipating a better tomorrow for yourself or for your loved ones can motivate you to fight for justice or seek new solutions to old and vexing problems. When you consider the future, you learn to balance your desires for immediate gratification with a commitment to achieving a delayed but lasting good. The problem arises when getting what we want becomes our reason for living and we enlist God as the guarantor of our desired future. Again, this is wishful thinking. Hope, much more than wishful thinking, gives us the power to persevere and the stamina to endure. But hope involves a different understanding of God and our circumstances.

5

Many of the Bible's stories teach us to trust in God's promises about our future. For instance, God promised childless Abraham and Sarah—themselves already well past childbearing age—more offspring than there are stars in the sky (Genesis 15:1-6). With some serious struggles and moments of doubt along the way, Abraham and Sarah trusted God. Sarah gave birth to Isaac in her very old age, and Israelites through the generations came to see themselves as the children of Abraham and Sarah. Similarly, when the people of Judah found themselves conquered by the Babylonians and enduring captivity in a distant empire, the words of Isaiah came to them, promising a messiah who would lead them out of bondage (Isaiah 9:6). But let's be honest. It's likely that Abraham and Sarah were wishing for babies to bounce on their own knees. Adulation by a nation of strangers centuries in the future was probably not what they had in mind. And Jesus was not the messianic figure that many of his contemporaries had come to anticipate. I mean, if you were looking for a warrior-king like David to rid you of the Roman occupiers, Jesus, the parable-slinging rabbi who was crucified, would have been a major disappointment. In other words, God doesn't seem to be in the business of fulfilling anybody's actual wish list. Nevertheless, sometimes we can approach God as if this is precisely how God operates—at least for those who *really* believe. We strike a sort of faith bargain with God: *If I believe, then God will deliver for me.*

Like my fellow bishops in the Episcopal Church, I travel to a different congregation most Sundays of the year. These congregations are scattered around my part of Louisiana, which is everything but the "toe of the boot" formed by our state's land mass. Farmers and lawyers, plumbers and nurses, students and retirees talk to me about how life is going. Sometimes they tell me that they have filed for divorce or that they are grieving a spouse's death. They may be struggling with a child's addiction or still looking for a job after months of unemployment. Most often it's when people are sharing stories of uncertain times, heartache, and disappointment that they tell me they're sure God has a plan. Often, this is just shorthand for saying that they trust the loving God to carry them through life's rough patches. Their struggles won't have been in vain, and they will grow spiritually by enduring them in faith. This attitude is not what I mean by wishful thinking. Instead, we engage in wishful thinking when we think of our faith as our part in a transaction with God. That transaction goes like this: If we believe tenaciously and fervently enough, God will reward us with the result we want. Mind you, our desired outcome may be something very good: a job to support our family, the healing of a child, or the mending of a troubled marriage. There is nothing wrong with wanting our circumstances to improve. But wishful thinking is a poor substitute for biblical hope.

Wishful thinking makes us susceptible to feeling let down, abandoned, and betrayed by God. From there, it's a short walk to bitterness, cynicism, and despair. Perhaps you can relate. You and God had a bargain. Or, at least, you thought that you had struck a deal with your Maker. All you wanted was to be happy. Nothing flashy. You didn't ask to be a billionaire or a fashion model or a Nobel prize winner. Just a roof over your head. Well, and maybe a garage, a new-ish car, a good job, a loving spouse, and well-adjusted kids. But still, you were just shooting for the kind of comfort and security that's pretty common for the American middle class. Surely God, being a loving Creator, not only wants you to have a good life but also promises to secure it for you. All you have to do is stick to the right set of theological beliefs, walk the line morally, and worship the God who made you. Even the rough patches in life are merely intermediate steps on the way to the final destination of happiness. Just keep the faith, and God will get you where you want to go. Only, that's *not* how it has worked out for you. You've kept the faith, and everything has fallen apart anyway . . . and it's not getting any better. You've lost your job, the bank has foreclosed on your house, your spouse has skipped town with someone else, and your kids have joined a gang.

Or let's say you're a faithful Christian who becomes terminally ill—nobody's idea of a happy ending. Clinging to the wishful-thinking version of hope puts you in an intellectual bind. You could say that God is punishing you for something you're unaware of or for some error in your beliefs, despite the fact that you have been a devout and caring follower of Jesus. Just consider what such thinking would be saying about God—that moral failings or faulty theology could provoke God to strike you dead, leaving your family and friends heart-stricken. Yet, the Bible tells us that God is love (1 John 4:8). It's very difficult to square such a violent, devastating action with the picture of a loving God. Actually, it seems to be a slur against God's enduring character. But even if you could somehow convince yourself that giving you a deadly illness was loving, think about the kind of tenuous hope with which such a scenario would leave you. Your hope would always be infected with an anxiety-producing "if." God will come through for you—if you are faithful enough. Sincerely prayerful enough. Theologically correct enough. Morally upright enough.

As for me, I've always got room to grow. For that matter, I manage to make mistakes pretty much every day. So I would constantly wonder if I were doing enough to fulfill my end of the bargain with God. Wishful thinking would leave me insecure about God's love for me precisely because that love would be a reward for something I do or accomplish. God's attitude toward me would depend upon flaky, sometimes grumpy, often clueless me. I would keep looking over my shoulder and asking, "So, God, are we still cool?"

No, I cannot bring myself to think of God as an executioner. But I do see why some people might feel uneasy hearing me suggest that something could happen without God's explicit input. Once you allow exceptions to the idea that everything happens for a reason—once you admit that some things are not part of God's plan—you have introduced the idea that we live in a cosmos where sometimes things just happen. Perhaps there is no divine plan that will make moral and spiritual sense out of the tragedies, injustices, and heartbreaks that happen every single day. If there is to be any such thing as hope in a world where things don't always make moral or spiritual sense, we'll have to find it in something other than a divine guarantee of a happy ending, which is precisely what I'm saying. We need a shift in thinking about hope. Hope is a visceral confidence that life is worth living. And that makes hope a matter of life and death.

A Reason to Live

The scenario we just considered is the sort of thing that makes writer Mark Manson want to be your barista. Before handing over your triple, venti, half-sweet, nonfat, caramel macchiato, he wants to pen a little note on your cup that would read like this:

> One day, you and everyone you love will die. And beyond a
> small group of people for an extremely brief period of time, little
> of what you say or do will ever matter. This is the Uncomfortable
> Truth of life. And everything you think or do is but an elaborate
> avoidance of it. We are inconsequential cosmic dust, bumping
> and milling about on a tiny blue speck. We imagine our own
> importance. We invent our purpose—we are nothing.[1]

Essentially, Manson says that the universe doesn't care about you at all. Things don't happen in your life to make you a better person, to teach you a lesson, to connect you with the spouse of your dreams, or to score a prime parking spot for you at the grocery store. The universe remains stubbornly indifferent to whether or not you get a promotion or make it through brain surgery, get the winning lottery ticket or survive a concentration camp. Stuff just happens.

Manson and I agree that we are hardwired to yearn for a reason to live. We disintegrate emotionally when we can't discern a "why" for all that we do. But, as he sees it, there is no such thing as a "why" in this universe of ours. He says that if we're going to survive, we have to make one up. So, we tell ourselves that the future will be better than the present. Whether it's through technological advances, political ideologies, natural laws, historical forces, or religious beliefs, something out there will make our life worth living by ensuring a happy ending. We only have to make a bargain with, or adhere to the dictates of, or be on the right side of that external power, and everything will come up roses. An anticipated future makes the present—whether merely mundane or dismal—worth enduring.

But what happens when you can't believe the comforting lie that a better tomorrow makes life worth living today? Here's what the philosopher Albert Camus says: "There is but one truly serious philosophical problem, and that is suicide."[2] When wishful thinking loses its hold on us, we move from asking *how* to stay alive to *why* we should stay alive. Camus tells the story of Sisyphus to illustrate his point. Angered by Sisyphus's pride, the gods condemned him to roll an enormous rock up a hill for all of eternity. Just as Sisyphus would reach the crest of the hill, the rock would roll back to the bottom. He would have to trudge down the hill and begin pushing from the starting point all over again. And again. And again. That's what a hopeless life looks like if hope is equivalent to wishful thinking. No matter how hard you work or how clever you are, nothing you do makes life any better. The gods could imagine no harsher punishment than the misery of an inescapably pointless life. Unless Sisyphus found something other than the anticipation of a happy ending to give him a reason to live, such a life would be unbearable.

We frequently use the word *despair* to refer to the kind of hopelessness the gods intended for Sisyphus. But a friend introduced me to a German word that I find evocative: *Weltschmerz*. You can translate the word literally as world-pain, but it's more aptly rendered as world-weariness.[3] It suggests that to inhabit this planet, simply to breathe the atmosphere, has become impossibly-heavy lifting. It's more than a momentary disorientation, anger, or sadness. *Weltschmerz* is an all-consuming spiritual exhaustion—a visceral sense that maybe, just maybe, life is unbearable; that this life might not be worth living. Have you or someone near to you ever felt this kind of world-weariness?

As a pastor, I've sat with many families through the emotional and spiritual aftermath of suicide. Survivors struggled with why their husband, wife, son, daughter, mother, father, sister, or brother took their own life. The best I've been able to offer in these situations is to be present with people in their grief, listen to their words, and abide with them in their silence. In most of these experiences I've sensed that when people ask "why," they're not merely seeking the cause for the suicide. They already know that their loved one was addicted to heroin or depressed or exhausted by chronic pain. Instead, they are expressing an ache. They recognize and yet cannot comprehend that nothing in this world—including their love for the one who has died—gave their loved one a reason to keep going. How could this be?

Most of us realize that our circumstances in and of themselves cannot make us happy. Yet, our responses to the suicides of popular celebrities or distinguished business leaders reveal that we have not entirely dismissed the idea that career success, material comfort, and admiration from others would make for the good life. One death that especially baffled me was the suicide of Anthony Bourdain, who was at the top of his professional game when he took his life. His show *Parts Unknown* was a hit. He was in love with a smart, capable woman. It appeared that the world had given him every reason to live. Still, Bourdain decided that his life was too heavy to bear. Countless essays and blog posts asked, "Why did Bourdain take his own life?" But as I reflected on his death, I realized that there is a more fundamental question. Each of us answers this question—usually tacitly and without reflection but sometimes with intentional passion—every time we get out of bed and lean into a new day: *Why should I keep living today? What am I really living for?*

Sometimes we confuse living with surviving. We all have a survival instinct. We are driven to find food and shelter, for instance. It's as automatic as breathing. Provided that we avoid a terminal illness or a catastrophic accident, we continue to survive until the wear and tear of advanced age finally takes us. Paradoxically, suicide shows us that living is more than surviving. We need to have something worth living for, a "why" that gives us a reason to persevere. Nobody else and nothing out there in the universe can give us such a why. *We* have to choose it for ourselves. Each day we are choosing whether to live or die, even if we do it passively and without much serious thought. It may come as a surprise to know that the Apocrypha says the same thing. For instance, Sirach says, "Before each person are life and death, / and whichever one chooses will be given" (Sirach 15:17, Apocrypha). As we will explore in the next chapter, Jesus teaches us that we make the choice to live when we choose to love. Loving makes life worth living, giving us hope, because in loving we connect with God.

Though Bourdain did not share his personal struggles with us, nutritionist Tara Condell gave us a tender glimpse into her inner life through her final blog post, written before she ended her own life at the age of twenty-seven. Her words reveal her world-weariness.[4] She wrote that her life looked enviable "on paper," but her world felt hollow. She acknowledged that there was much she loved about this life: "Real true authentic street tacos . . . unexpected hugs . . . the Golden Gate Bridge at sunset . . . saying I love you . . . shooting the shit." And yet she was "tired of feeling tired." Even though she recognized the incontestable goodness of many people, places, and things, none of them gave her the "why" she needed to carry on living. So she said goodbye. No tragedy, cruelty, or disappointment had led her to leave this life. There was simply no other option for her. "Shikata ga'nai," she wrote. *It cannot be helped.* Nothing can be done about it. She said, "I have accepted hope is nothing more than delayed disappointment." She had seen through the illusion of wishful thinking. Life was not too heavy to bear but, for her, too empty to endure.

Condell's words suggest that, without something worth living for, she was ending her life because "it's time for me to be happy." She seemed to be saying that by dying, she would be escaping this dreary world and transitioning to an infinitely better one. Toward the end of that final post, she added a message to her deceased father: "I'm coming home, Dad. Make some room up on that cloud and turn the Motown up." Rather than inspire her to endure this life or to lean into it with grit, the afterlife seemed to offer her an attractive alternative to this world. Sometimes we, as Christians, can subscribe to a similar perspective when we embrace wishful thinking rather than a biblical concept of hope.

Hope and Eternal Life

When you hear the words *eternal life*, do you think first of traveling to a different spiritual location or going to heaven? Even if we believe in life after this life, the anticipation of a better hereafter is not what gives us real hope in the here and now. Just as I believe hope is vastly better than wishful thinking, I believe eternal life is greater than going to a place called heaven when we die. Some would say that the purpose of human life on this planet is to go to heaven, which is paradise. There you will never know pain, sorrow, or death again. Heaven is a place of undiluted, undisturbed happiness. While some believe that everyone goes to heaven when they die, others view this life as a proving ground or a trial for the next life. Many Christians hold that if we believe in Jesus—and some would add that if our faith is expressed in good works—then the pearly gates will swing wide for us. Hell awaits everyone else. In this line of thinking, the prospect of getting into heaven motivates our life on planet Earth.

By contrast, let us consider another idea—that eternal life is the kind of existence we begin to inhabit as we enter into relationship with Christ in our ordinary, everyday lives. In relationship with God, over time, we become our true selves. God's love saturates and transforms us. Because we are the beloved, our daily lives take the shape of love, and this kind of life has an eternal trajectory. No tomb can contain it. Eternal life has no end but begins right here on planet Earth. That's because this is where God first embraces us. That's one of the lessons of Jesus's birth. Our hope rests on the idea that God loves us so much that God will come to dwell where we are. Whether it's in a crummy neighborhood in a backwater town like Bethlehem, an elementary school classroom, a field of wildflowers, or a concentration camp. God comes to where we are. God shows up in the kindness of strangers and friends, and God's presence changes everything. God's presence makes this life worth living. The Revelation to John expresses it this way: "The home of God is among mortals. / He will dwell with them; / they will be his peoples, / and God himself will be with them" (Revelation 21:3).

In her memoir *Everything Happens for a Reason: And Other Lies I've Loved,* Duke Divinity School professor Kate Bowler takes us along for the ride as she struggles personally to find hope in a world that offers no guaranteed happy endings.[5] At the age of 35, doctors diagnosed her with Stage IV cancer. In her earlier book, *Blessed,*[6] Bowler had closely studied not only the theology but also the spiritual lives of Christians who subscribe to the prosperity gospel: the belief that God rewards the faithful in this life with health and wealth. While she had had affection and respect for the people she came to know during her research, she had rejected the idea that hope is the anticipation of a God-given happy ending. After her diagnosis, Bowler recognized that her intellectual rejection of what I call wishful thinking had left her with spiritual work of her own to do. But she didn't look toward heaven for a way to make her life worth living. Instead, she found hope of a kind that sounds remarkably Jesus-y to me. She found it in the people she loves and those who love her. In her love for her son and her husband. In the prayers, the casseroles, the hand-holding, and the simple acts of kindness offered by friends and strangers, coworkers and family. She found it in the divine love that passes in and through other people right here in this life. And that love, I believe, is the beginning of eternal life.

Hope, you see, is more than even the most faith-infused wishful thinking. It is the sense that life is worth living because love dwells within us and pours out from us—a love that has the power to make life worth living.

THE POWER OF LOVE

*To be loved, and to love, need courage, the courage to
judge certain values as of ultimate concern—and to
take the jump and stake everything on these values.*

—Erich Fromm, *The Art of Loving*

When Joy and I returned to the hospital room, our daughter, Meredith, was sitting up in bed sipping apple juice with a straw. Puffy, her lovingly battered stuffed rabbit, was tucked under one arm. A Barney video was playing on the TV. Every nurse in the Pediatric Cardiac ICU surrounded her bed, laughing and clapping.

At just eighteen months, Meredith had undergone open-heart surgery. Following her physician's instructions, we had left the room while they took her off the ventilator. The weeks-long buildup to the surgery, the hours of waiting for the procedure to be over, and finally the helpless agony of watching her terrified eyes plead with us to remove the tube from her throat had left us knackered. The relief and joy we felt at seeing Meredith holding court with those nurses was a welcome contrast to the dread and emotional nausea that had been churning within us.

Joy told one of the nurses how touched we were that they had turned that moment into a celebration. The nurse responded with something like, "Oh, thanks! But honestly we did that as much for us as for her. You see, most of our patients are so little and so sick. The surgeries don't often turn out this well. Celebrating her good result helps keep us going." Joy and I had been sustained by the idea that the surgery would make Meredith whole and that all would be well. The prospect of a happy ending had kept us going. At the nurse's words, I looked up as if seeing where I was for the first time. What I observed suggested an entirely different kind of hope, a hope derived from something other than the anticipation of a happy ending. Down the hallway, exhausted, emotionally weary parents sat attentively by the bedsides of tiny babies hooked up to monitors, IV drips, and ventilators. Their children would be going home to face still more surgeries, struggle with chronic physical limitations, and celebrate a mere handful of birthdays. Some realized that their little one would pass their final hours in that hospital. And these mothers and fathers kept going. No happy ending in sight. These parents taught me that hope begins by acknowledging "It is what it is" *and then* leaning into what actually is with all your heart.

It Is What It Is, Now What . . . ?

You may be puzzled to hear a bishop—or any follower of Jesus—say that hope rests on the admission that "it is what it is." After all, I believe in a good and loving God. I've staked my life on it. So you might reasonably expect me to say that God heals our wounds, cures our sicknesses, sets things right, rewards the just, and gives the wicked their comeuppance. You also might assume that when life seems unfair, I will defend God. Get God off the hook for cooking up the unpalatable moral stew that this world all too frequently is. I'm used to it. People look to me to explain how this benevolent, omniscient, omnipotent God could let babies die and good parents bear unimaginable grief. I've spent years thinking, writing, and teaching about how to reconcile the concept of a loving God with the cruel realities of this world, first as a philosophy professor and then as an ordained

THE POWER OF LOVE

leader in the church. While reflecting on what people often call "the problem of suffering" can be fruitful, I've come to believe that the randomness of suffering presents us with a more fundamental, terrifying challenge—not for the intellect but for our very existence. Is life really worth living in a world that doesn't make moral sense? In a world where there is frequently a disconnect between who we are and what we do on the one hand and the prospect of a happy ending on the other? A world where stuff just happens?

As we discussed in the last chapter, many of us resist the idea that stuff just happens. God has a plan, we say. Everything happens for a reason. In other words, the world makes moral sense because God blesses the righteous and punishes the sinful and the unfaithful. We just can't quite make out how that all works. That's what Jesus said, right? Well, actually, not so much. Jesus bluntly tells us that the universe deals each of us an apparently random hand. In the Sermon on the Mount he says, "[God] makes his sun rise on the evil and on the good, and sends rain on the righteous and on the unrighteous" (Matthew 5:45). Law-abiding, hardworking people lose their homes in tornadoes, wildfires, and hurricanes. Innocent children are born with defective hearts and develop cancer. Conversely, notorious crime bosses live long, prosperous lives. Self-absorbed jerks inherit enormous fortunes, congratulate themselves on their unearned wealth, and blame poverty on the laziness of the poor. Moral uprightness, spiritual devotion, and even the innocence of youth don't appear to give anybody an inside shot at a happy ending on this planet.

Jesus is painfully honest. Life is an imperfect gift. Wonderful and wretched things happen. "It is what it is." Only, that's not where he stops. He basically says, "It is what it is. Now what are you going to do about it?" Hope begins by squarely facing reality: It is what it is. But we are capable of doing more than merely acknowledging, passively accepting, or blindly reacting to the contours and dynamics of the world we inhabit. This is where the implied "now what" of Jesus comes in for us. We have the radical freedom to choose to love.

Jesus makes our freedom to choose love especially clear in one of his most counterintuitive teachings: love your enemy. Again and again we will encounter people who use coercion, violence, and domination to make a better place for themselves in the world at the expense of others. It's tempting, maybe even appropriate by some people's estimate, to hit back. Fight fire with fire. By contrast, Jesus teaches us to inhabit this planet in a fundamentally different way. We can refuse to be enemies even, and especially, with those who insist on seeing us as their enemy. Instead, we can choose to actualize our true selves as the image of God, as the "children of your Father in heaven" (Matthew 5:45). As we've said, God is love. So when we love, it is God's love pouring into us, saturating us, and overflowing from within us. That's how the living God is present with us and in us. Receiving love and freely choosing to give that love away make life worth living, giving us the "why" to keep going in the world as it actually is.

Nothing can prevent us from choosing to love. We are radically free to do so. Conversely, nothing compels us to love. We must choose to live for love, to make love the driving force of our lives. That's why Jesus presses us to challenge ourselves with this question: "On what am I staking my life?" It could be love. Or power. Or prestige. Or possessions. For instance, Jesus calls two people to follow him as he makes his way to Jerusalem and, eventually, to crucifixion and resurrection. The first person agrees but asks to bury his father first. "Let the dead bury their own dead," Jesus says. The second asks simply to say goodbye to family members. Jesus responds, "No one who puts a hand to the plow and looks back is fit for the kingdom of God" (Luke 9:60-62). Here Jesus is urging them to be honest about the "why" of their lives and whether or not this "why" will sustain them in even their darkest hour.

Jesus never misled his followers with the promise that love would be easy or would guarantee desired outcomes. But he did emphasize the importance of perseverance. Just keep going, he tells us. Consider the parable of the unjust judge. There's a corrupt, self-serving judge notorious for padding his own pockets and pursuing his own interests at the expense of, well, pretty much everybody else. A woman petitions this judge for justice. Initially, he ignores her. But her persistence is Guinness-Book-of-World-Records kind of stuff. We might say she texts him, trolls him on social media, turns up at his doorstep, throws pebbles at his bedroom window, and loiters outside his office door. Finally, he grants her petition just to get her off his back (Luke 18:1-8).

Obviously, God is not the self-absorbed jerk that this judge represents. We might think Jesus is going to say that if a guy like this will give this woman what she wants for her persistence, then surely we can count on the loving God. Right? Pray hard and long enough and we'll get what we want. But here's a news flash. God is not a vending machine, and prayers are not coins we stuff into the slot to get the candy we want. Just in case we don't get the point, Jesus tosses out this gem: "Will not God grant justice to his chosen ones who cry to him day and night? Will he delay long in helping them?" (Luke 18:7). Um, well, actually, Jesus, we are crying out to God day and night. And as a matter of fact, there's been quite the delay. Like, you know, centuries upon centuries of delay. Suffering and sorrow litter the planet. Why doesn't God fix it?

I can't tell you why God doesn't fix everything. This parable doesn't explain that. But it does tell us to persevere. To keep going. And here's why: It's what God would do. It's what God is doing. It's what we do when we are our truest selves, the image of God. We love. We love in specific ways. Sometimes we're heroic. We sacrifice a career or our reputation by daring to speak up for the oppressed or the marginalized. Mostly we're ordinary and routine. We bring casseroles to the bereaved or we babysit for an exhausted single parent. Whatever form our love may take, we love with our hands and our feet. It is what it is right here and now, *now what* are we going to do about it—rather than resign ourselves to the state of things? We do something because we believe that love does what nothing else can.

What Love Can Do

When he was only two, Jean-Paul's father died. His grieving mother returned to her family's home, where she raised her son with the cheerful help of her sisters. The women fussed over little Jean-Paul and dressed him in the toddler fashions of *fin de siecle* France. Think Little Lord Fauntleroy. Knee breeches. Shirts with large, embroidered linen collars. Long hair elaborately curled, draped over his shoulders, and flowing onto his brow.

His grandfather watched on with silent disdain for what his daughters were making of his grandson. Eventually, the old man got his chance to put at least some things right. He learned that his daughters had decided to enjoy a day trip together. Once the women were well on their way, Jean-Paul's grandfather sheared off those heavy locks and cropped the boy's hair close to his scalp. As evening approached, the women returned. Jean-Paul ran eagerly to greet them. Their reaction stunned him. At the sight of him, they gasped in horror, burst into tears, and fled from the room.

Stunned and confused, the toddler gazed at himself in a mirror. Years later, Jean-Paul recalled that this was the moment that he realized that he was ugly. His mother and aunts had grown his hair long to hide his exotropia, or misaligned eye. He had been born with one eye that always turned sharply to the right. The medical science of the time provided no effective treatment. That little boy grew up to be the famous twentieth-century existentialist philosopher Jean-Paul Sartre.

My teacher and friend Tom used to tell this story to illustrate how Sartre understood human freedom.[1] We are all free to make choices at every instant of our lives, yet none of us is free to choose the circumstances under which we will make those choices. The concrete details of life limit the kinds of choices we can make and the impact that those choices can have. Sartre called this *facticity*. As for me, I prefer the term that his German contemporary Martin Heidegger used: *thrownness*. Each of us is thrown into a world not of our own making. We did not choose our parents, our DNA, or the nation of our birth. We did not choose the economic class or the political system into which we were born. For centuries others have been shaping the world's economies, political systems, social structures, and climate. We're left to muddle through the world that they've left for us. It is what it is. We're thrown into injustices, absurdities, and ongoing catastrophes not of our own making.

I think the idea of thrownness is a helpful way to talk about the Fall. The story about Adam and Eve does not have to point to primordial parents who made lousy choices. Neither do we have to follow Augustine's odd notion that original sin passes from parents to children because the parents had sex. Nope. The Fall is the idea that we are free to make choices in a world shattered in ways not of our own making, a world that is at once breathtakingly beautiful and hideously scarred. Our spiritual challenge is to walk in love in a way that might heal, mend, and even transform our circumstances.

That, I think, is precisely what Jesus is getting at in the parable of the dishonest manager (Luke 16:1-13). Here's my retelling: People have reported to a rich man that his portfolio manager is ripping him off. So, the rich man calls his manager in and gives him a pink slip. Scrambling to soften his own landing, the manager runs around town to all the people who owe this rich guy a debt, letting them know that he has cooked the books in their favor. He has shaved the amount of their debts, figuring they'll owe him one later. The rich guy finds this out, but instead of getting angry, he splits a gut laughing and takes the manager out for a drink. The manager is his kind of guy. That sort of shrewdness is how you get ahead in this world.

Jesus flatly acknowledges that we live in a world where unscrupulous, self-serving people frequently exercise immense influence, reach celebrity status, and accumulate heaps of cash. Exploitation, manipulation, and coercion actually get results with distressing frequency. Observing the success, prestige, and comfort achieved by the world's most cunning people, we can be tempted to be what some might call "realistic." To play the world's game by the rules of the shadiest and most ruthless among us.

21

Yet, Jesus urges a different course. Don't be naive, he says. Acknowledge how this world so often works, and then trust the power of love to change the world's very DNA.

In his royal wedding sermon, Episcopal Church Presiding Bishop Michael Curry drew on Pierre Teilhard de Chardin's analogy of love to fire. Teilhard reminded us that the discovery and harnessing of fire had radically changed the world. Fire makes all travel possible, whether by car or truck, train or plane. Lose the fire and you're sitting motionless in a hunk of metal. Without fire, there would be no telecommunications. No internet. No electrical devices.

By comparison, the love of God in Christ will transform this world. God's love will flow through Christ's hands and feet. As it turns out, those hands and feet are ours. Through us, God's love can restore, heal, and liberate this aching, shattered world. Here's what Bishop Curry said about love in that sermon: "There's power in love. There's power in love to help and heal when nothing else can. There's power in love to lift up and liberate when nothing else will. There's power in love to show us the way to live."[2]

In Greek mythology, the gods jealously guarded the secret of fire. It was the key to their status and power. Looking down from Mount Olympus, the Titan Prometheus saw that humans were weak, naked, and afraid. In compassion, he shared fire with humans. Enraged by Prometheus's betrayal, Zeus chained him to a rock and sent an eagle to eat out his liver every day for eternity. Clearly, fire was meant to be solely a divine privilege. But our God is not a petty, selfish god who stockpiles treasures and jealously guards them for personal use only. God holds the key to life, freedom, and hope. That key is love . . . which God gives away to everyone like some drunken sailor on liberty. God has no preconditions. There are no strings attached. But God yearns for one thing above all else: that we would give that love away just as prodigally as God does.

This is why God sent Jesus to live in our midst: to show us how to love with abandon, setting us on the path to remaking this world with God's own power—with love. Bishop Curry challenges us to imagine the world that God will make when we follow Jesus's way of love:

> When love is the way—unselfish, sacrificial, redemptive
> love—then no child will go to bed hungry in this world
> ever again. . . . When love is the way, poverty will become
> history. . . . We will lay down our swords and shields . . . to
> study war no more. When love is the way, there's plenty good
> room . . . for all of God's children.[3]

Swept up by God's redeeming love, we cannot help but be moved—not just in our emotions, but in our actions. Some of us will be stirred by compassion for the sorrows and sufferings that lie heavy on this world. Others of us will be set in motion by righteous anger at the injustices crushing so many of God's children.

When we choose Jesus's way of love, we display an initial enthusiasm for God's dream of a redeemed world. Works of love pour out of us, even when that work is arduous and costly. Eventually, fear may grip us. We may grow weary. But neither fear nor exhaustion presents love its greatest challenge. No, the greatest challenge to living the way of love is time. The arc of justice is long. We frequently wait years, even centuries, to see the result of love's power. In some seasons, we experience a resurgence of hate, fear, envy, and violence—as if love has finally lost the day. We can grow discouraged and cynical. If we had only our own inner resources from which to draw, we might tumble into bitter resignation. But thankfully we are not alone. God is in this messy life with us. And God's loving presence is the ultimate source of hope—a hope that is eternal.

God's Love Is Eternal Life

We didn't know that her name would be Marie. We didn't know that she would be a she. Before the era of sonograms, my mom was massively pregnant. Three-year-old me wanted a baby sister. So, with Mom's help,

I grabbed a crayon and wrote Santa a letter asking for just that. My memories from that age are gauzy and piecemeal. I remember writing the letter and leaving it on the front stoop of our shabby duplex. I remember eagerly anticipating a baby sister. And I remember Mom telling me that Marie had died.

Marie's death shattered my mother and left me frightened and confused. To console me, my mother said that Marie was in heaven. One day we would see her again. Many of us—Christians and non-Christians alike—find comfort in the idea of life after death and the prospect of reuniting with those we love but see no longer. Frankly, so do I. But, as I have explained, the thought of heaven does not, at least for me, make life worth living. Instead, my hope stems from an awareness of and an intimacy with God in the course of normal, everyday life. Admittedly, my connection with the Holy comes and goes in intensity and clarity. Frankly, sometimes Netflix gets more of my attention than I like to admit. Nevertheless, through my connection with God, the deep algorithms of my existence begin to shift toward eternal life—or what I call a resurrection-shaped life.

Consider what Jesus once said about the resurrection. In his day, as in ours, there were competing views about life after death. Luke records an exchange that Jesus had with the Sadducees, who did not believe in the resurrection of the body and offered an argument intended to show that accepting the idea of the resurrection leads to logical absurdities (Luke 20:27-32). Jesus responded with this: "The fact that the dead are raised Moses himself showed, in the story about the bush, where he speaks of the Lord as the God of Abraham, the God of Isaac, and the God of Jacob. Now he is God not of the dead, but of the living; for to him all of them are alive" (Luke 20:37-38).

God loves Abraham, Isaac, and Jacob because, well, that's who God is. God is love, and to be the God of anyone or anything is to love. But God's love is not mere affection. God's love is the power that brings the entire universe into being, the power that sustains you and me in each and every instant. And, as Jesus pointed out to the Sadducees, God's love is eternal. The divine love is the power that sustains life beyond the grave. Receiving and imparting God's love is eternal life, a life that changes but does not end when we draw our last earthly breath. Eternal life, then, is a love relationship with God and, through Christ, with all of God's creation.

This is such good news: receiving love from the eternal lover and giving that love away begin here on planet Earth. God is present in and through the entire creation. It is not necessary to wait until we die to meet our Maker. God reaches out to us, embraces us, and transforms us from the womb to the grave and every point in between. That is why some of us refer to dying as entering into the "nearer presence" of God. In death, we anticipate seeing with greater clarity what we glimpse now only dimly. Yet it is this dim glimpse from which we draw the hope that sustains us in this life. God is with us. Always and everywhere. Throughout the creation. And it is the risen Jesus who makes this so.

PART II

The God Who Shows Up

Hope is not about proving anything. It's about choosing to believe this one thing, that love is bigger than any grim, bleak shit anyone can throw at us.

—Anne Lamott, *Plan B: Further Thoughts on Faith*

3

GOD WITH US

And above all, watch with glittering eyes the whole world around
you because the greatest secrets are always hidden in the most
unlikely places. Those who don't believe in magic will never find it.

—Roald Dahl, *The Minpins*

My wife, Joy, and I live in Central Louisiana. Amid the bayous and the pine forests lie cultivated fields of corn, milo, sugar cane, and cotton. People cluster in small towns or, like Joy and me, live in homes scattered around the unincorporated countryside. Mockingbirds and hawks fly overhead. Fox, deer, and feral hogs roam the woods. Snakes slither through the underbrush, and alligators swim the waterways. Insects are everywhere.

In June and July, first light brings deer flies. They attack anything that moves, delivering a painful bite to feed on their prey's blood. Once they've identified you as part of a nutritious breakfast, no amount of swatting deters them. Even if you run, they pursue you for what seems like miles, buzzing around your head and torso. To avoid being harassed and stung, Joy and I gulp down a cup of coffee, throw on our walking gear, and hit the wood-lined paths before sunrise. Dawn usually breaks behind us on the final stretch of our hike, so flies pester us for the last half mile or so. They target our dog, Gracie, first. To rescue her from them, Joy rushes ahead to get Gracie back inside the house. On one such morning, as

Joy was hurrying up our driveway, she looked back at me and shouted, "Turn around!"

At first I thought, "Are you kidding? These deer flies are gnawing my arm off!" But after a moment's pause, I looked back. The sun itself had not yet come into view. Gauzy strands of cloud glowed pink and red across the horizon. Light appeared to be shining from within them, not merely upon them from some distant source. Involuntarily I muttered the universal prayer of the wonderstruck: "Wow." It's what we say—audibly or inaudibly—when something has taken our breath away. As Anne Lamott puts it, "'Wow' means we are not dulled to wonder."[1] Wonder is the beginning of hope.

Love and Wonder

"Wow" is a common expression. We use it in a variety of ways. Sometimes we're acknowledging somebody's good news. "I got an A in my Organic Chemistry class!" "Wow!" We react to horrors and absurdities with, "Wow! That's awful!" or, "Just, wow!" But the "wow" I uttered in response to that sunrise was of a different variety, the kind that expresses a state of wonder. I gasped with my whole being as I saw a beauty that conveyed something spiritual to my heart and soul. This sort of "wow" is more than an autonomic response like saying "ouch" when you stub your toe. The vastness of the sea, the majesty of a mountain range, or the timbre of a singer's voice moves you in a deep and enduring way. The moment usually passes quickly, yet it's as if a tectonic shift in your self-understanding and perception of the world around you has begun, if only in some small way. That's because God has addressed you. And God always addresses you with love. That's when God begins to be real in your life.

One of my philosophy students taught me this lesson years ago. We'll call her Hulga. Like her parents and grandparents, Hulga was culturally Jewish and devoutly agnostic. She was bright, articulate, and wickedly funny. During a classroom discussion about one of the classic proofs for the existence of God, Hulga offered an insightful criticism of the thinker's line of reasoning. She ended by saying something like, "There's really no evidence that persuades me to believe in God."

I responded playfully, asking her what she would do if God showed up in this classroom and, in a booming Wizard-of-Oz sort of voice said, "Kneel and worship me." Without missing a beat, she said, "I would say forget it. Just look at the mess you've made. Besides, that's no way to start a relationship."

Then I asked her to consider another scenario. God sits next to you, looks you in the eye, and says, "I love you." Hulga grew silent and thoughtful for several long seconds. "I've never thought of that," she said. "That would be really different." I think she meant, "Wow!"

The kind of "wow" I'm talking about is like being caught in God's gaze. You know what it's like to be caught in the act of doing something when you thought no one was looking. Maybe you were talking to yourself or scratching your rear end and you heard a cough or footsteps behind you. You've been seen. Someone else makes themselves known to you, but you don't see them. You're being seen by them. Wonder is our experience of being seen by the God who is love through and through. God's love does more than merely acknowledge our lovableness. God's love makes us the beloved. Wonder is the realization that we are the beloved, and this is where hope begins.

My "wow" in response to the morning sky was more than a merely aesthetic reaction to beautiful colors and the play of light. God's love felt palpable. I'm not claiming to have had a vision of God or to have heard God's voice with my ears. Nor am I suggesting that we will lay our eyes on the divine as if God were just one more mockingbird or pine tree in our line of sight, and I readily admit that I'm talking about highly personal, unrepeatable experiences that could never count as scientific data or proof of the existence of God. Still, I experienced myself as God's beloved. We were created to yearn for and be fulfilled by God's love for us. As Augustine put it in *The Confessions*: "You have made us for yourself, and our heart is restless until it rests in you.[2] We say "wow" when God's love embraces us from within the world we inhabit.

Some may balk at the idea of looking for God in sunrises, wildflowers, or barn swallows. These are creatures, after all, not the Creator, who surely dwells beyond this world in heaven. Perhaps you've had or encountered similar thoughts. I realize what I've been saying about wonder may sound as if I have been praying to one of God's creatures—like the glowing morning sky—instead of praying to the God who made it. If that were indeed what I had been up to, then I would have been participating in idolatry: putting something less than God in the place that only God can genuinely occupy in my life. So, let me be clear. God is the source of authentic hope. What I am saying is that this hope arises in our ordinary lives from our everyday encounters with the God who dwells in the midst of this world with us. As it turns out, the story of Creation actually teaches us that God resides at the heart of all things.

God at the Heart of Things

When we read the Genesis story, we often interpret it to say that God created everything out of nothing (though according to Genesis 1:2, God moved over the deep). In other words, in the beginning there was God. No time. No space. No internet. No Starbucks. Just God. So God's way of creating the universe bears no resemblance to how I assembled the IKEA desk in my wife's study. I screwed and hammered together a bunch of already-existing parts. But God spoke, and the cosmos came into being out of absolutely nothing. God set both natural and human history into motion with a word: "Let there be light" (Genesis 1:3). And because God is merciful, I imagine that word was followed swiftly by, "Let there be coffee."

Saying that God created everything out of nothing means that God is God and the creation is not. In a sense, there is a bright red line that distinguishes the Creator from created things. Every dog, black hole, peach tree, and cicada came out of nothing and, without God, would collapse right back into it. Everything is dependent upon our Maker. The Maker of all things needs nothing else to exist. This is what theologians call *transcendence*. God is separate from and independent of the creation. Yet, these same theologians teach us that God is also *immanent*. God dwells within the creation without being a created thing. Admittedly, the idea that God is both transcendent and immanent is a paradox. How can God be both beyond and within? Separate from and one with the universe? We might respond to this paradox by emphasizing, even perhaps unwittingly, God's transcendence over God's immanence. God's distance over God's closeness. We might feel comfortable saying that God is in our hearts and resist saying that God dwells at the heart of all things. So, in our thinking we end up placing the Maker over there and the created universe over here.

This line of thought is similar to the idea that God is like a great clockmaker, argued by philosopher and clergyperson William Paley (1743–1805). If you or I stumbled upon an intricate apparatus like a clock on some deserted beach, we would have to conclude that it could not possibly have assembled itself or come to be there through mere chance. Its complexity points beyond itself to a clockmaker. Likewise, nature is remarkably complex and intricate in its workings. So, by analogy, there must be a Maker for the whole universe. There must be a God. While philosophers have pointed out the logical problems of this argument, it's the spiritual implications of Paley's idea of God that concern us here. God stands at a distance. Once the clockmaker completes the timepiece, it ticks away all by itself. The clock is not intimately, perpetually connected to the maker. Someone designed the clock, wound it up, and left it to run on its own. An observer merely infers a distant maker from the clock. To borrow an image from writer and scholar Diana Butler Bass, Paley's proof leaves us with a God so distant that God needs an elevator to get down to us from heaven.[3] So it is no surprise that when we emphasize God's transcendence, we must draw our hope from beyond this world. A distant God is working out a plan. Life in heaven will compensate for or vindicate the sorrows, suffering, and disappointments we encounter on Earth.

By contrast, medieval theologian and mystic Meister Eckhart (1260–1328) wrote, "The Father speaks the Son out of all his power, and he speaks in him all things. All created things are God's speech."[4] Did you catch that? All created things are God's speech. Every rock, tree, crawfish, and cranky toddler. In case Eckhart seems to be stretching the Christian envelope too far, consider Paul's letter to the Colossians. He and Eckhart are on the same sheet of music. Paul writes, "For in him all things in heaven and on earth were created . . . all things have been created through him and for him. . . . And in him all things hold together" (Colossians 1:16-17). Similarly, mystic Hildegard of Bingen (1098–1179) writes of the creative power of God's love burning in the depths of all things: "Thus I am concealed in things as fiery energy. They are ablaze through me, like the breath that ceaselessly enlivens the human being, or like the wind-tossed flame in a fire. All these things live in their essence, and there is no death in them, for I am life."[5]

God's relationship with the creation is analogous to that between artists and their work. Artists pour themselves into their work—writers like Anne Tyler and Charles Dickens and composers like Nina Simone and Ludwig van Beethoven. In their fiction and in their music, these artists convey something of themselves, something of their interior lives, to their readers and to their listeners. In a similar way, God pours God's self into the creation. Longleaf pines, fireflies, wood ducks, and cynical teenagers glimmer with the divine love. A love that does more than pull creatures out of the hat of nothingness and then admire them from a distance. A love that dwells within them and reaches out beyond them to the rest of creation. What does this mean for us? We can encounter God's love for us not only in the interior chambers of our own hearts but also in the depths of all that surrounds us.

Wonder is the response of our whole being to that encounter with the divine, whether we meet God in a sunset, a starry sky, the Holy Sacrament, the lines in an old person's face, or the immensity of the sea. Philosophers like Immanuel Kant have used the word "sublime" for these sorts of experiences. When a finite being crosses paths with the infinite, when an incomprehensible magnitude stretches to bursting all the limits we place on our thinking and our feeling—wow! We don't have the words, and we are not the same after such an encounter. But being stretched by the infinite is only part of the story. Wonder reveals to us that we matter to this infinitely good, beautiful, and powerful being. The divine has brought us into being and sustains our existence as an act of inexpressible love.

When I was a boy in a small town of the Deep South, I would sit on our back stoop as dusk settled into night. Slowly, the fireflies would come out. At first a few and eventually scores of tiny lanterns would gently fade on and off, each to its own rhythm. Gradually, my heart's heaviness would lift and my racing mind would grow still. Those twinkling lights instilled in me a sense of the deep goodness and beauty of the trees, grass, cicadas, and my own life. I was a pudgy kid. Others often bullied me because of a speech impediment. My family was disintegrating. My father alternated between charm and violence. Our shabby house sat next to a junkyard. Yet, in those moments I felt life's sweetness. My life seemed worth living because I was loved. In just such a moment is where hope begins.

Some might understandably object, saying that hope comes from Jesus, not from stars, rose bushes, and mockingbirds. We know God's love in Jesus. He is God incarnate, and he died for our sins. I don't dispute that Jesus gives us hope. On the contrary, that is precisely what I am saying. The risen Jesus is the source of our hope, and this does not contradict what I've said thus far about encountering the divine in the midst of our ordinary lives. Yet, I realize my understanding of why God became a human being—and how Jesus relates to God's creation of all things—may seem like "coloring outside the lines" of a more widely held view. At least, that's what my experience has shown me. But do you know what I've discovered? Coloring outside the lines helps me to see the wonder of the risen Christ.

The Wonder of the Risen Christ

My clerical collar, black shirt, and black suit were drawing discreet glances. I had slipped away from the church office to get some cold medicine at a nearby drug store. The checkout line turned out to be unexpectedly long. A man standing in front of me glanced over his shoulder, took a double take, and then whirled on me. Without the slightest hint of irony and sounding remarkably like a homicide detective interrogating a likely suspect, he asked, "Are you saved?"

Stunned that my outfit hadn't clued this guy in to my vocation, all I could think to say was, "What?"

"Are you saved?" he repeated. "Do you accept Jesus Christ as your Lord and Savior?"

"What?" No longer stunned, I was now on guard against a potential cross-denominational assault.

He went on to ask me if I knew where I would be going when I die. "We're all sinners. If sinners don't repent, they go to hell. And you never know when the Grim Reaper will show up. Don't wait until it's too late. Accept Jesus now so you know you're going to heaven." He continued like that without seeming to take a breath. The line slowly inched forward. Finally, he stopped when the cashier said, "Is that all, sir?" She took the words right out of my mouth. After paying, he shoved a small comic book–like tract into my hand with the admonition, "You better read this before it's too late!"

The tract he handed me outlined a familiar narrative. God created the world. It was good. Perfect. Flawless. The first humans—Adam and Eve—lived in the Garden of Eden under one simple rule. Eat whatever you like except for the fruit of the Tree of the Knowledge of Good and Evil. Succumbing to the wiles of a serpent, Adam and Eve ate the fruit. God expelled them from paradise. By their sin they fell from grace, and humans have been saddled with sin ever since. The just punishment for sin is death. God is just. But God is also merciful. So in response to human sin, God sent

Jesus to pay the price for our sin. Jesus is God's response to human wickedness. If we accept Jesus on these terms, we are saved and enjoy the hope of eternal life in paradise. Jesus is God's fallback plan for creation.

By contrast, Franciscan theologian John Duns Scotus teaches that Jesus was not God's reaction to sin but God's first thought in creating all things, because God's motive for creation is love. God yearns to be in seamless union with the creation. Jesus was God incarnate: God and human at once perfectly distinguished and yet inseparably intertwined. God's purpose in creating the universe was to love all things with an infinite, inextinguishable love. Up close and personal. The risen Jesus is the crowning achievement of the creation. He is the same as and yet infinitely more than the Jesus who walked the streets of Nazareth two millennia ago. Christ actually inhabits and animates every earthly body. That's what thinkers like Richard Rohr mean by the phrase the "Universal Christ"— Christ present in all things and in all people.

The risen Jesus taught us that he would be present to us in a new and profoundly intimate way as he emerged from the empty tomb and revealed himself to his first apostle: Mary Magdalene (John 20). (Because an apostle is one sent to proclaim the Resurrection and Mary Magdalene brought the news of the risen Christ to the men we usually call apostles, she is sometimes called the apostle to the apostles.) As she approached in the predawn gloom, Mary realized that something or someone had rolled away the stone sealing Jesus's tomb. Without investigating further, she hurried back to the disciples to report what she had seen. Peter and John raced to see for themselves. Mary kept pace with them but drew up short as the two men reached the grave. Peering into and finally entering the tomb, Peter and John found it empty but for the burial cloths. The two men returned home, mulling over what they had experienced, while Mary lingered a while longer.

Finally, Mary leaned in to take a look. Unlike the men, she found the tomb inhabited by two angels. It seems that she wasn't startled by them because she carried on a conversation with them as if seeing heavenly beings in an empty tomb was as common as passing a familiar greeter at the entrance of a store.

They noticed her sobbing and asked, "Why are you crying?"

She said, "I see no body." She came looking for Jesus, but she saw nobody.

As she turned around, a stranger—she assumed he was just a gardener—asked her, "Whom are you looking for?"

"I'm looking for Jesus, but I see no body."

Mary was looking right at the risen Christ, and yet she saw nobody. For her, the gardener was nobody. And here lies the first lesson that the risen Christ wants us to learn: the risen Christ is different from, and more than, the pre-crucifixion Jesus of Nazareth. This is a lesson about him and a lesson about us.

You see, before his death and resurrection, Jesus could be only one body in one place. If you were looking for him in a crowd, you were playing a real-life version of Where's Waldo. He was just one face among many. But the risen Christ resides in time and space without being limited by them. He can eat fish and offer his hands to be touched (John 21:12; 20:27). Yet he can pass through locked doors (John 20:19), appear and disappear before our eyes, and travel the distance from Emmaus to Jerusalem in a mere instant (Luke 24:13-36). We will find him even, and perhaps especially, in the stranger, in the very one we tend to see as nobody. Jesus's challenge to us is to recognize him.

I suspect that each of us has experienced being somebody and being nobody. Being seen and being overlooked.

Years ago, I participated in an advanced philosophy seminar in Perugia, Italy. Everyone there had received a doctorate or was nearing completion of the degree from one of two distinguished universities and had known each other previously—except for one woman and myself. She was teaching at a European institution, and I was studying at another university. In our free time on a Saturday afternoon, she and I sat together on a patio looking across the Umbrian hills at Assisi. Several of our fellow participants wandered up, chatting animatedly with each other. They glanced at us but continued their conversation among themselves.

One of them said, "Where is everybody?"

Another said, "Nobody's here." They strolled off toward town without acknowledging us.

After a moment of looking into the distance, my colleague turned to me and said wistfully, "I wonder what it would take to be somebody."

The good news is that everybody is somebody. The risen Christ dwells in each of us, in you and in me. Seeing this truth famously led St. John Chrysostom to say, essentially, that you do not revere Christ in the bread and the wine of the Eucharist if you do not honor him in the poor, the orphan, and the widow.[6] Christ dwells in each and every person—he touches through their skin, sees through their eyes, hungers with their bellies. Each homeless teenager, hardened inmate, desperate refugee, and detained child is somebody. And what's more, the risen Christ's presence is not restricted to human beings. Like the beautiful sunrise that elicited wonder in me, the risen Christ resides at the heart of all things. Though he is not reducible to or the same as wildflowers and mountain ranges, the starry sky or the vastness of the ocean, he reaches out to us from within all things precisely because they were created through him and for him. Finding the risen Christ in our surroundings is our vocation as people of the Resurrection. It's like learning to color outside the lines.

But let's face it, sometimes our actual circumstances don't feel so stinking wonderful. Suffering and violence pervade our world. God's presence is anything but obvious. Picturesque beaches, majestic peaks, healthy babies, and moonlit nights can move us emotionally and even inspire us to compose romantic music or write lyrical poetry. But our world is not all moonbeams, kittens, and rainbows. Lions feast on gazelles, alligators devour beloved pets who wander too close to the bayou, and powerful humans prey upon and abuse the vulnerable. Even so, this world is where hope begins. I believe hope begins in the midst of, and sustains us within, what Mary Oliver called "the great and cruel mystery of the world."[7] Frederick Buechner summarizes the prophetic message of the Hebrew Scriptures like this: "Here is the world. Beautiful and terrible things will happen. Don't be afraid. I am with you."[8] In other words, through the prophets God admits that life is going to be messy. It's going to leave a mark. But we should hang in there. God promises to be in it with us and, together with us, make a difference. Or, as Jesus says, "I am with you always" (Matthew 28:20). In fact, Jesus himself told us to look for God in precisely the places of suffering, deprivation, and oppression. It was Bobby McFerrin who sang, "Don't worry, be happy,"[9] not Jesus. Jesus said, "If any want to become my followers, let them deny themselves and take up their cross and follow me" (Matthew 16:24). As we do, we will discover that God dwells with us even in the midst of suffering and violence, shining an inextinguishable light.

An Inextinguishable Light

May it be a light to you in dark places, when all other lights go out.

— J.R.R. Tolkien, *The Fellowship of the Ring*

After dinner, as the sun sank below the horizon, my mother would spread a blanket for us on the grass in our backyard. I had not yet entered kindergarten, and this routine served as part of my bedtime ritual. We would lie side by side, gazing silently upward. One star, and then another, and then several at once would twinkle amid the deepening gloom. Eventually, billions of stars dusted our little patch of earth with a gentle light. A serenity settled into our bones. When clouds hid the stars from us, my mother would say, "Remember, those stars are still shining down on you, even when it's hard to see them."

Whether my mother initially intended for our nightly stargazing sessions to be lessons in hope or not, that's how they seem to me looking back. She did not speak to me about hope as a theological virtue. Instead, she helped me to feel hope for myself. Passing clouds provided her with a teachable moment. Life is not all starry skies and moonbeams. Sometimes it will enrage you or leave you breathless with grief. Storms blow in, and if we lose sight of the deep goodness and beauty of the world, we can tumble into despair. So, she seemed to be saying, keep looking for the holiness all around you. Or, as I've come to say it now, look for God in messy places, in the life you've actually got. Hope bubbles up from an awareness that God is in this mess with you, offering light in the darkness. But God is doing more than merely sitting alongside you. God's love is making you what Paul called a "new creation" (2 Corinthians 5:17). This is resurrection at work in your life, a process of dying to an old life and rising to greater life already in process on planet Earth.

A nominal Roman Catholic, my mother was spiritual but not religious before that way of identifying yourself became common. She trusted God implicitly, not as a fixer-in-chief who guarantees positive outcomes but as a reliable, sustaining, nurturing presence. As the one who would be with her and love her no matter what—and whose love would continue to shape her into her true self. I suppose that's why she loved with nearly reckless abandon, and I've come to see that her relentless hopefulness arose from her awareness of what God was doing in her life. God's relentless love for her led her to devote her own life to loving others. She hadn't learned this lesson from the nuns at school or from the pulpit during Mass but, as I mentioned in the introduction, from her experience as a prisoner in Mauthausen-Gusen Concentration Camp.

Hope in a Hopeless Place

Mauthausen-Gusen was actually a complex of concentration camps. The main camp rested atop a hill outside the village Mauthausen, about twelve miles from my mother's hometown of Linz, in Upper Austria. The complex included nearly one hundred sub-camps. Three of these sub-camps lay near Gusen and, combined, sometimes housed more prisoners than the main camp. Mauthausen was a work camp. Auschwitz-Birkenau and Treblinka were death camps. But these terms are deceptive, because the mission of both work and death camps was the same: extermination. Only the method and the speed of execution differed. Death camps centered on gas chambers and ovens. Once prisoners arrived at these camps, guards and kapos quickly gassed and then cremated them. In work camps, execution occurred slowly through a deliberate and deadly combination of long hours of exhausting labor, starvation rations, and squalid living conditions. Guards regularly beat prisoners to death for failing to work diligently, for a missing button on their tattered uniform, or merely for the sadistic pleasure of it. The camp's administration reserved the gas chamber for those who fell too ill or too weak to continue working. Because the likelihood of dying in Mauthausen was especially high among the concentration camps, Nazi bureaucrats in Berlin referred to the camp as the "Bone Grinder."

In the spring of 2019, Joy and I visited Mauthausen for the first time. Its granite walls, imposing guard towers, barracks, gas chamber, and ovens now stand as a memorial to honor those who suffered and died in that ghastly place and to prevent the rest of us from forgetting. The site's administration provides a personal guide for family members of former captives, and our guide Rupert did more than walk us through the physical plant of Mauthausen. He led us, as best he could, through my mother's experience there.

My mother, Trudy, arrived in the village by train just as 1944 was edging into 1945. She would soon turn sixteen. At the station, SS guards brutally rushed the prisoners from their cars and herded them through the town's streets. As the frightened, weary captives shuffled and stumbled along, Mauthausen's citizens went unperturbed about their ordinary rounds. There was no jeering or staring. There were no furtive, compassionate glances. The arrival of prisoners was such a commonplace experience that they were invisible, too insignificant to cause revulsion or contempt. They were nobody. By contrast, the residents warmly greeted the guards. Shopkeepers and Hausfraus and bankers smiled and waved at them. Called out to them cordially by name. Swapped jokes and issued invitations. "Hans, remember dinner at 8:00! My daughter can't wait to see you!"

The contrast of this atmosphere to my mother's home—a mere twelve miles to the west—must have been staggering to her. Only days before

43

she had strolled down similar streets lined with bakeries, cafes, and parks. People had called out to her by name, slipped her a fresh roll still warm from the oven, or flashed her a friendly smile. They would have recognized her. She belonged to that place. To those people. But as soon as she arrived in the village of Mauthausen, she belonged nowhere. No address, neighborhood, family, or schoolmates. The intended message was clear: "You matter to no one. You are neither loved nor lovable. Your life is insignificant. It's not worth living."

A steep mile-and-a-half slog brought my mother and her fellow inmates to the camp's imposing gates. Immediately upon entering the camp, guards forced the prisoners to march to the right until they came to a rough stone courtyard hemmed in by the wall and an administrative building. The Nazis called this area the "Wailing Wall." There, guards ordered everyone to strip, to toss their clothing and any additional belongings in a pile by the building, and then to turn and face the Wailing Wall. Prisoners trembled at attention. Naked, humiliated, and terrified. After standing interminably in the cold and enduring capricious blows to their heads, legs, and backs, the captives were ushered into the basement of the building. Other inmates crudely shaved their heads with dull razors. For delousing, everyone was jammed into an adjoining room with dozens of shower heads jutting from the ceiling. When they emerged disoriented and demoralized, they donned ill-fitting striped uniforms—most of which had been reclaimed from deceased inmates— and were fitted with a bracelet bearing a number that replaced their name.

In this place, under these dreadful circumstances, my mother developed a mature hope. You might think that her liberation taught her to hope. After all, she was there on May 5, 1945, when the 11th Armored Division of the US Third Army rolled up to the main camp. To the day of her death, my mother remained deeply grateful to the soldiers who rescued her from that place. However, the substance of my mother's hope was not that God would eventually get her out of whatever awful jam she might find herself. Instead, she felt that life was worth living because God was with her.

She decided to keep living every day. Some of her fellow prisoners decided to end their lives by suicide. Life for them had become unbearable. By contrast, my mother's hope remained unextinguished because of the light, however dim, of God's presence with her.

My mother spoke very sparingly about the details of her time in Mauthausen. She was especially reticent about sharing the spiritual struggles and emotional impact of her imprisonment. I know only the barest outlines of her inner journey and how her awareness of God's love provided for her a life-sustaining light in that dark, brutal place. As a way to understand that experience more fully, I turned to another young woman's story to understand *how* someone might find life worth living in the camps simply by recognizing God's presence. Etty Hillesum's journal entries— and the accounts of her life given by survivors who knew her—give us a glimpse into a person animated by a life-giving awareness of God's loving presence. And it was from that awareness that she, like my mother, derived an inextinguishable hope.

A Life-Giving Awareness

Etty Hillesum was twenty-six when the Nazis invaded Holland in the spring of 1940.[1]

At the time, she was in the midst of intensive psychotherapy. Initially, her diaries continued to focus on her own emotional struggles. Her entries treated the occupation indirectly as merely the external setting for her own internal drama. Around two years after the invasion, her therapist— who had also become her lover—died of cancer. After his death, her diary entries reveal a gradual spiritual awakening. Her spirituality was personal rather than formally religious. She became aware of God's presence within the depths of her soul and in the world around her. She wrote, "Suddenly I knew deep down how someone can sink impetuously to his knees and find peace there, his face hidden in his folded hands."[2] In the midst of prayer, she writes, "All personal ambition drops away from me, and . . . my thirst for knowledge and understanding comes to rest, and a small piece of eternity descends on me with a sweeping wingbeat."[3]

The Nazis began systematically rounding up Jews in April of 1942. Families were arrested and shipped away on trains, never to return. Rumors spread about concentration camps and gas chambers. Understandably, Etty thought first of her own safety and retreated from the world in prayer. By July, however, her response to the Nazis had changed. "They are out to destroy us completely, we must accept that and go from there."[4] But she refused to react to the Nazis' brutality by mirroring their hate and violence. Instead, she responded with love to the suffering and sorrow wrought by the occupation.

Twenty-five thousand of her fellow Dutch Jews went into hiding. Eighteen thousand of them survived. By contrast, Etty chose to remain and bring whatever comfort and healing she could. Eventually, she volunteered to work at Westerbork, the transit camp from which one hundred thousand Dutch Jews were eventually shipped to the Auschwitz gas chambers. She went from bed to bed in Westerbork's four hospitals tending to the sick and the dispirited. In letters written to their families, other Westerbork inmates described her as warm and radiant. She became for them an emblem of love and a source of hope. Etty writes to a friend,

> The misery here is quite terrible; and yet, late at night when
> the day has slunk away into the depths behind me, I often walk
> with a spring in my step along the barbed wire. . . . I can't help
> it, that's just the way it is, like some elementary force—the
> feeling that life is glorious and magnificent and that one day we
> shall be building a whole new world.[5]

In September of 1943, Etty learned that the Nazis would be shipping her and her family to Auschwitz. She had no illusions. This was a death sentence for them all. And yet, she persevered. Here is how her friend Jopie

Vleeschhouwer described Etty as she prepared to leave for the death camp: "Talking gaily, smiling, a kind word for everyone she met on the way, full of sparkling good humor, perhaps just a touch of sadness, but every inch the Etty you all know so well."[6] While some may doubt the sincerity of Etty's demeanor, seeing it as a brave front or as massive denial, the larger context of her diaries and letters suggests something else. She experienced in herself and in the lives of those she loved an "elementary force," a life that is "glorious and magnificent," even when facing certain death.

Crammed into a cattle car on the way to the death camp, Etty wrote a postcard and shoved it through the cracks as the train rolled down the tracks. Remarkably, farmers found that postcard and sent it along to Amsterdam. The note read, "Opening the Bible at random I find this: 'The Lord is my high tower.' I am sitting on my rucksack in the middle of a full freight car. Father, mother and Mischa are a few cars away. . . . We left the camp singing, Father and mother firmly and calmly, Mischa too."[7] Her hope arose not from the sense that God would dramatically rescue her from the Nazis; she understood that death awaited her and her family at Auschwitz. Instead, Etty's hope was her felt sense of God's abiding presence, even in the most dreadful circumstances. God was traveling along with her in that cattle car. God would be standing naked in the gas chamber as she entered. Etty not only understood but experienced that God inhabits every corner of the creation, whether beautiful or terrible. Because God is with us, nothing and no one can strip us of our true identity as the beloved and as one who loves. On November 30, 1943, Etty died in Auschwitz. But until her final breath, nothing could extinguish her hope. To use the words of John's Gospel, "The light shines in the darkness, and the darkness did not overcome it" (John 1:5).

While Etty Hillesum's story is stirring and inspiring, it would be a mistake for us to conclude from her example that hope is a spiritual *achievement*. Still worse, it would be a brutal lapse in compassion to condescend to those who tumble into despair for lack of faith—as we all do at one time or another. The life of faith on this planet includes not only glimpses of the divine but also moments in which God seems to have left the building. A loved one dies suddenly, a marriage dissolves, a diagnosis rocks us, or a cherished dream turns to dust. The world goes dark. After Mother Teresa died, we learned from her personal journals that she had felt God's absence for years. Even Jesus cried from the cross, "My God, my God, why have you forsaken me?" (Matthew 27:46). In Jesus, God meets us wherever we are, including where we feel godforsaken—our places of deepest despair. Jesus's words teach us that we do not generate our own hope by having a deep prayer life, following rigorous spiritual practices, clinging tenaciously to our theological convictions, or adhering strictly to a moral code. Hope is not something we accomplish. Hope is a divine gift. As such, God does not judge us or forsake us when we fall into despair. On the contrary, God keeps showing up. Even in the tomb.

Struggling with Despair

The call came at 7:30 in the morning. A level yet authoritative voice asked, "Is this Father Jake Owensby?" This couldn't be good. And it wasn't. Continuing in a matter-of-fact tone, a police officer informed me that a man—we'll call him Ned—had shot himself. He had pinned a note to his jacket with my name and phone number and instructions that I should be called to handle his estate and conduct his funeral. He had walked out of his apartment to the adjacent parking lot, sat in his Jeep, closed the door, placed a shotgun under his chin, and pulled the trigger.

Ned had been in recovery for around a year, and I was serving as his sponsor. Bright, creative, and articulate, Ned had gotten sober after a dismally low bottom. Alcohol had wrecked his body, destroyed his once promising career, and ruined him financially. Surviving on the dwindling remains of an inheritance, he resisted taking any of the jobs available to him. To do so would have forced him to accept his significantly reduced prospects, diminished circumstances, and tarnished reputation among former peers.

While I was his sponsor, he had relapsed once and, together, we had climbed back out of that hole. He seemed to have turned a corner. But in retrospect, I realize that he had slipped into despair and resigned himself to death. The life he led no longer felt worth living to Ned, and he didn't want any of us who knew him to short-circuit his plan to take his own life.

In the homily that I preached for Ned's funeral, I reminded people that we would be reciting the Apostles' Creed as part of the service. The contemporary version of the creed reads that Jesus "descended to the dead." By contrast, the traditional version contains the words "descended into hell." I suspect all of us know a little bit about being in one kind of hell or another. Loneliness. Self-loathing. Fear. Rage. Resentment. Feelings of failure, abandonment, and betrayal. It's like being sealed in a dark and airless tomb with no way out.

The message of Jesus's life is that God doesn't just follow us wherever we go. In Jesus, God is there before we arrive. Jesus died on a cross, and his friends buried him in someone else's tomb. Even though Joseph of Arimathea owned that specific burial site, it stands for each of our own graves. Jesus precedes each of us into our darkest place, into our hell, and that's what I believe he did for Ned. In the depths of his darkness, even after he had taken his own life, I think Ned discovered that he was not alone after all. I imagine that as Ned passed from this life to the next, he found that Jesus had preceded him into the tomb—and in time, that Jesus would ask him, "What's a nice guy like you doing in a place like this? Let's get the hell out of here."

Again, hope is not an accomplishment that gives the spiritually elite bragging rights. The lesson of Etty Hillesum's life is not that a few extraordinary spiritual giants can find God in unlikely places and make themselves love other people no matter what. Instead, her experience and her remarkable capacity for hope demonstrate that hope is the gift that God gives by showing up and leaning into whatever beautiful scene or wretched mess we find ourselves in. I believe that God gives this gift to everyone.

You may ask why, if this is true, some people never seem to sense God's presence and very few can claim to be continually aware of the God in our midst. I do not know. But the stories of ordinary people encountering God in their everyday life continue to inspire me to keep my eyes, my heart, and my mind open. Maybe that's true for you, too.

In the little classic *The Practice of the Presence of God*, seventeenth-century monk Brother Lawrence says that God is always present—in all things and all places. He writes that we feel life's worth when we discern that presence and radically surrender ourselves to it, in the mundane and in the glorious, in the sublime and in the hideous. Practicing God's presence is more than setting aside a time and a place for prayer. Instead, Brother Lawrence urges us to recognize that everything we do in life can be a prayer, because prayer is simply offering ourselves to the Divine. Whether we are preparing a meal, washing clothes, repairing a car, or singing in a church choir, we can offer that activity—and hence, ourselves—to God. For Brother Lawrence, the goal is to make all of life a continuous prayer. Then, in what may seem a paradox, this radical devotion to God in all things actually deepens and amplifies our relationships with others. In his preface to one of the many editions, Henri Nouwen puts it this way:

> Brother Lawrence's life shows clearly his great openness for his
> fellow human beings. He reminds us in a forceful way that we
> cannot find God in people but that it is God in us who finds
> God in people. When we are concerned with God and God
> alone then we discover that the God of our prayer is the God
> of our neighbor. Therefore: The closer we come to God, the
> closer we come to each other.[8]

In other words, when we love God with all our heart, soul, mind, and strength, we will end up loving our neighbor—the neighbor whom God loves. And our love of neighbor will deepen our awareness of the God who is with us, the God who shines light in the darkness.

Looking for Light

When our now-adult children were little and the Christmas season rolled around, we would pile into the car after supper and ride around, looking at Christmas lights. We deliberately chose neighborhoods whose streets were lined with glittering homes and yards dotted by illuminated crèches, snowmen, and festively dressed Snoopys. Cheerful gasps, thrilled giggles, and shouts of "Look! Look!" spilled out of the back seat as we rolled along. The way those lights pierced the dark cast a spell on all of us back then. Honestly, it does the same to me still, even though my post-sunset drives during the Christmas season are now mostly solo. On these shortest of days I am usually traveling home from the office or finishing the day's rounds, and the neighborhoods through which I pass are frequently not those we would have chosen those many years ago.

One night at Christmastime, I drove through a familiar part of town where shotgun houses lined the dimly lit streets. In these shotgun houses, a single door opens to a hallway that runs down the center of the tiny wooden-frame structure to the back door. Cramped rooms lie on either side of the interior passage. Peeling lead-based paint or battered asbestos siding inadequately seals the exterior walls. Renters furnish their stoops with the shabby love seats and rickety office chairs they've retrieved from trash heaps littering the curb, evidence of their neighbors' evictions.

House after house retreated from my sight into the gloom. Then, ahead to my left, green and red flickered in the corner of my eye. I slowed to see a strand of lights rimming the frame of the single window and another strand around the door of the house. Those few lights cast a deeper spell than even the ones I had known in years past. As Luke teaches us, heaven bends low to touch the earth—to infuse it—with the glorious presence of God: among scruffy shepherds in a mucky field and in an over-full hostel in a crummy backwater of the world's largest, most dangerous empire (Luke 2:1-20). God joins us even in the midst of our gloom. The gloom of poverty and racism. The gloom of loneliness and grief. The gloom of family dysfunction and addiction. The light shines. God is there. God is with us. And the gloom cannot extinguish it.

When I got to the office the next day, I looked up the origin of shotgun houses. I had always heard that they got their name from that central hallway; people had said that you could shoot a gun straight through the house from front to back without hitting a thing. Hence, shotgun house. But what I learned in my brief research showed me that what I had heard was mistaken, and it transformed the shotgun house into an icon of hope.

Some scholars believe that the word "shotgun house" is actually a corruption of the West African term for this type of dwelling. Slaves originally built these cheap, practical dwellings in what is now Haiti. They brought the design with them to New Orleans when their owners relocated. These slaves called this kind of dwelling a "shogun," which means "God's House."[9]

Those slaves knew in their bones that, despite their cruel captivity and harsh treatment, God dwelled with them. To live at all is to live with God in their midst. So to live can be a profound act of resistance, resistance against the forces of this world that would imprison, impoverish, diminish, harass, and oppress the children of God and resistance that refuses to be extinguished and chooses to be light in the darkest gloom. God sent Jesus into this world. The address that God chose for Jesus's birth was not Palatine Hill, one of the most prestigious neighborhoods in ancient Rome. Instead, Mary gave birth to her baby boy in a humble building whose address was so obscure that FedEx probably wouldn't have found it in time for Christmas. In Jesus, we see that God comes to dwell in the midst of gloom. God comes not merely to provide the comfort of a little light to those who happen to believe but to be the inextinguishable light that once and for all dispels the gloom—in all its forms—that too often hangs over the beloved children of God. This is the Incarnation. Love come down to dwell among us. And this is the source of our hope.

PART III

Remember That You Are Called

I think it would be well, and proper, and obedient,
and pure, to grasp your one necessity and not let it go,
to dangle from it limp wherever it takes you.

—Annie Dillard, "Living Like Weasels"

PART
III

5

HOPE AND CALLING

Discovering vocation does not mean scrambling
toward some prize just beyond my reach but
accepting the treasure of true self I already possess.

—Parker J. Palmer, *Let Your Life Speak*

"Don't confuse your job with your vocation."

William said this to me while we were sitting in his study during one of my monthly spiritual direction sessions. I confided to him that I was struggling. Even though the congregation I was serving had begun to grow rapidly, opposing groups argued with each other about what sort of music we should sing. A few grumbled that I wasn't spirit-filled enough. Others wondered aloud about my orthodoxy. Some murmured that I was too Catholic. It was all starting to feel pointless, and I was ready to quit.

In seminary, our professors had frequently reminded us that churches are likely to be no less dysfunctional than your average family. To apply what Anne Lamott has said about the various tribes to which we belong, congregations work because not everybody is crazy at the same time.[1] A few hearty souls keep everybody moving forward while the rest of us busy ourselves offloading our anxieties and disappointments in the form of quarreling, gossiping, and complaining. At the time of this session with William, I hadn't been a priest long enough to have made peace with the realities of life in religious community. Instead, the constant sniping, carping, and backbiting were beginning to wear me down. While I can't remember my specific words to William that day, I'm sure they came down to something like this: I'm discouraged. Sometimes I just want to walk away. How do I keep on going?

William saw my struggle for what it was: a crisis of hope. That's why he said, "Don't confuse your job with your vocation." He understood and helped me begin to get my head around the idea that hope involves a clear, abiding sense of your vocation, or calling. You might hear in the word *calling* or *vocation* some job or cause that you feel born for. You might think of Dorothy Day's commitment to social justice, Jane Goodall's work with primates, or Stephen Hawking's search for the underlying principles of the universe. Perhaps you've understood a calling to be some big thing you're supposed to pursue or do with your life or else go unfulfilled. It's the organizing principle for everything you do.

But actually, I don't think this is what William had in mind when he challenged me to double down on my vocation, and that's a good thing. As the writer Emily Esfahani Smith points out, most people will not experience a Jane Goodall–sized sense of calling. If having hope required that sort of vocation, most human beings would spend their lives sinking into despair. Instead, Smith writes, "The world is full of retail clerks, coupon sorters, accountants, and students. It is full of highway flaggers, parents, government bureaucrats, and bartenders. And it is full of nurses, teachers, and clergy."[2] Many of these people experience their lives as profoundly worth living. Smith argues that, instead of a vocation, they have found a purpose. They don't derive hope from their job itself. Rather, the job (whatever it may be) provides them "opportunities to help others."[3] Smith's distinction between vocation and purpose is a helpful one. Nevertheless, I believe that what she calls "purpose" is precisely how we should understand the deeply imbedded, God-given calling that all human beings share.

My struggle had arisen in part because I believed that being a priest was my vocation. William helped me see that being a priest (and now being a bishop) is how I live out my vocation, but my calling goes much deeper than my ordained ministry. My calling—and yours—is to love God by loving what God loves, how God loves it. The risen Jesus said as much to Peter.

Jesus Calls. Again.

The apostles were fishing on Lake Tiberias. Enough time had gone by that the initial crisis of Jesus's death and the thrill of his resurrection have passed from vivid experience to clear-yet-receding memory. They're working stiffs making a living. Even though their own lives will never be the same after absorbing their friend's teachings, watching his crucifixion, and witnessing his resurrection, the world they inhabit has kept turning in pretty much the same way it had been before anybody had ever heard about Jesus of Nazareth. The apostles were wrestling with how to navigate a largely unchanged world as the radically transformed people that Jesus had made them. In the meantime, they do what they know how to do. They go fishing.

After a long night on the lake, the apostles had nothing to show for their efforts. Jesus appeared on the shore as the sun began peeking over the horizon. They didn't recognize him. He called out to them, "Caught anything?" They mumbled a grumpy, "No." Despite the fact that this stranger appears to know nothing about their lifelong trade, they followed the guy's advice to toss their nets over the right side of their boat. To their surprise, they pulled in a gigantic haul. That's when the beloved disciple, John, recognized Jesus and told Peter who it was who was standing on the shore. Apparently, Peter had been fishing nearly in the buff. The text tells us that he threw on his clothes, dove into the water, and swam a hundred yards to join Jesus on the beach (John 21:1-8).

As they all came ashore, they discovered that Jesus had already set a fire and begun preparing a breakfast of fish and bread. Jesus added some of their new catch to the grill and served his friends a huge seaside feast. With full stomachs and pleasantly bewildered souls, the friends relaxed in the sand, and Jesus turned to Peter for a conversation about vocation, the vocation Peter would share with the rest of the apostles, the calling we all share to this day (John 21:15-17).

The risen Jesus asked Peter, "Do you love me?" Not once or twice, but three times. Each time Peter said, "Yes!" And each time Jesus said some version of "Feed my sheep." You may recall that, on the night before the crucifixion, Peter had denied even knowing Jesus three separate times (John 18:15-27). Peter had abandoned, forgotten, or rejected his deep bond with Jesus in his terror, doubt, and confusion. Now, on this beach, Jesus was renewing Peter's call, a call grounded in Jesus's love for him. That's how our deep calling works. God keeps drawing us toward who we truly are, knowing full well that we'll forget, run from, or betray who we really are more than once. The very essence of God's call to Peter—and to the rest of the apostles, and to each and every one of us—is love.

The essential human calling is to love God by loving what God loves, how God loves it. We frequently refer to this as the Great Commandment or the summary of the Law. Jesus himself summarized the whole Torah by saying that we should love God with every ounce of our being and love our neighbor as if our own life depends upon their well-being (Matthew 22:34-40). Strictly speaking, this is our calling. When you hear the word *commandment*, you may think of an order issued or a directive given by an authority figure. If you refuse or fail to obey, negative consequences follow. You might begin to think that if we don't love, God won't love us anymore. But again, this is our *calling*. God's love attracts us, draws us toward love. God loves us because God's very nature is love. Love invites us into itself, to become one. Love invites us to be love and become our truest selves. So, our calling is to be the image of God in whatever occupation, situation, or set of circumstances in which we find ourselves. This is who we were created to be.

My spiritual director, William, had not been telling me that the priesthood was the wrong career for me. Neither was he denying that God had coaxed and nagged me into holy orders. Instead, his point was that the priesthood (and he would now probably say the episcopate) is the path by which I am working out God's calling to be a person who loves. Others have different paths. For that matter, my journey with Christ could one day lead me down a different road, a different sort of day job. But the vocation would not change. Conversely, even work devoted to worship, charity, peace, and justice can be nothing more than self-serving career tracks when they serve our desire for status, security, and influence. As I've heard Presiding Bishop Michael Curry frequently say, if it's not about love, it's not about God. I would add that if it's not about God's call to love, then it's not about vocation.

Experiencing a sense of calling brings with it the realization that your existence on this planet makes a difference. Think of it as your "George Bailey" moment. George Bailey is the protagonist of the classic Christmas film *It's a Wonderful Life*.[4] Facing scandal from a financial crisis not of his own making, George decides to take his own life. He leaps from a bridge into the icy waters below. An inept but kindly angel named Clarence rescues him from drowning and introduces him to a world with which he is completely unfamiliar: the world that never knew the small kindnesses and selfless generosity of George Bailey, the world as it would have been had George never existed. His beloved hometown was a meaner, bleaker place because he had never lived there. The people he had known as lively and joyful were guarded, irritable, or timid. George had been the president of a small, struggling savings and loan. He didn't pursue wealth, celebrity, or political influence. On the contrary, he drew a meager salary and lived modestly in order to put the bank's resources to work improving the lives of his hardworking, struggling neighbors through loans that other institutions would not risk.

Most of us will live quite ordinary lives in jobs we take to make ends meet. These jobs are not likely to offer us a great platform from which to change the world. However, in most every line of work, we encounter people. We brush up against Jesus's sheep, and we can feed them with our respect, attention, and kindness. For instance, my mother's last job was behind a deli counter in a grocery store. She greeted people by name and remembered their usual orders. Her focus was on making her customers' day better. She fed Jesus's sheep, and her attention to serving others was the source of her own hopefulness. Researchers would probably say that my mother had stumbled onto one of the keys to a fulfilling life. Devoting ourselves to helping others in our daily work makes that work, whatever it may be, seem worthwhile. We feel that we're making a difference. Emily Esfahani Smith writes, "No matter what occupies our days, when we reframe our tasks as opportunities to help others, our lives and our work feel more significant."[5] Or as Jesus put it, "Those who want to save their life will lose it, and those who lose their life for my sake will find it" (Matthew 16:25). Devoting our lives to the well-being of others—losing our lives—is a way of being ready for what we are all called to do: give ourselves back to God.

Being Ready

My friend John got a call one evening from the dementia unit. His father had been suffering from Alzheimer's for several years. John's father had dressed himself, packed his suitcase, and was now waiting in a visitor's lounge. The staff had tried to coax him back into his room. Each time he insisted, "They're coming to take me home." When John got there, he sat and talked calmly with his dad for a while. Eventually they walked together back to his room. After the older man fell asleep, John unpacked his dad's few belongings, thanked the staff, and drove home. The next evening, John got another call. The dementia unit again. This time, a nurse gave him the news that his father had died. When John had finished telling me about his father's death, he said, "I guess deep down he knew. He sensed that he was dying. They were coming to take him home. And he wanted to be ready."

Being ready for death is, paradoxically, the key to living a full, rewarding, and joyful life. I don't mean that we're most alive when we're bracing for our imminent demise. Rather, I'm talking about a habitual spiritual posture that comes with recognizing and embracing this life's finitude. Our earthly lives will come to an end. Our hearts will someday beat their last. We won't be able to take any of our accumulated treasures with us. For some people, this leads to the conclusion that you should eat, drink, and be merry while you can. But Jesus offers a different message.

Life is not about stockpiling things and chasing pleasure. It's not about getting applause, exercising power, or enjoying status. Life is about love, and love is about giving your life away. Mind you, Jesus enjoyed dinner parties and watching sunsets and laughing with friends just as much as the next person. Actually, more than the next person. That's because Jesus under-stood how to appreciate fleeting things instead of staking his life on them.

Everyone we care about and everything that gives us pleasure is a gift given to us for a season. One day, we will have to let them go. We will return these people and things to the one who gave them to us in the first place, and we will give our very own lives back to the one who gave them to us. In fact, all of life is preparation for giving our lives back to God. Followers of Jesus must let go because Jesus himself set the pattern of eternal life. That pattern is dying to an old life and rising to greater life, dying to a narrower self in order to rise to a broader, more expansive self. Honestly, letting go is probably our chief spiritual challenge. We let go of the familiar, of the life we know, for something that we can at best glimpse.

Perhaps even more distressing to us is the realization that life is a mysterious gift to be received, not a planned outcome that we can control. It's as if we turn over the authorship of our life to another writer, unsure of what the ending will look like. And this is exactly what Jesus tells his friends in Matthew 16:25. When we let go, we surrender authorship of our story to God. God writes our ending, but not the one we may have insisted upon or chased after. Jesus said, "If the owner of the house had known in what part of the night the thief was coming, he would have stayed awake and would not have let his house be broken into. Therefore you also must be ready, for the Son of Man is coming at an unexpected hour" (Matthew 24:43-44). Letting go is our contribution to the transformation that God offers us, from the earthly life we can make on our own to the eternal life we experience in relationship with God even now. This transformation is so radical that it's like turning stone into water.

How Stone Becomes Water

During my early twenties, I reached the height of what I think of as my wary cynicism phase. As far as I was concerned, the universe was populated by people and institutions who would eventually let me down. To be fair to my younger self, I was only just learning to navigate adulthood. My childhood memories of abuse, rejection, and exploitation were still open wounds. Perhaps unsurprisingly, these wounds announced themselves to me in nagging feelings of shame that occasionally erupted into turbulent, overwhelming storms. The anger I felt at those who had injured me had mutated into a persistent sense that I could never measure up. I was just no good. Admitting my inner turmoil and the injuries that gave rise to it felt too risky at the time. So, I adopted the posture of wary cynicism. To borrow from a phrase from the meerkat Timon of *The Lion King*, when the world turned its back on me, I turned my back on the world.

Eventually, somebody who knew me and cared about me said, "You are like stone. Be like water." For once, instead of dismissing what I heard with an internal eye roll, I stopped and listened. Something like this is what followed.

Consider what it's like to draw on a stone, on sand, and on water. Of the three, the stone is the hardest, the least vulnerable. Leaving a mark on the stone is difficult. You may need to use a hammer and chisel. As a result, marks left on the stone endure for a very, very long time. By contrast, sand yields more easily. If you've been to the beach, you know that with a rake, a shovel, or even a toe, you can draw all sorts of things on the sand. What you draw will last for a while, but it won't be permanent. Wind and waves will soon erase the marks you've made. Finally, you can draw on water with your finger if you like, but the mark you make disappears just as soon as you make it. Water remains open to the world and receives the world's influence even to its very depths. Water is moved, and yet, it is not disfigured. Water is always moving beyond what has happened to it.

In a moment of clarity, I realized that there is a different way to inhabit planet Earth. I was like a stone. My identity was bound up with my habitual resentment, bitterness, and sense of alienation. My wounds were defining me. Now I believe, because I have experienced it, that new life emerges from broken places. A new kind of life, not merely the next chapter of the old sort of life we lived previously. Stone becomes water. That's one metaphor that helps me understand the resurrection.

The apostle Paul characterized the resurrection as a physical body giving way to a spiritual body (1 Corinthians 15:44). Elsewhere, he said that in Christ we are a new creation (2 Corinthians 5:17). Paul had in mind both what happens to us after we die and how, in Christ, God's love radically transforms us right here on planet Earth. Hope is the visceral sense that God's love is actively shaping us into who we truly yearn to be. As we respond to the divine love, the deep logic of how we inhabit the world gradually changes, and we grow toward the loving model we see in Jesus:

- If someone steals your coat, you give them the shirt off your back (Matthew 5:40).
- You forgive the unrepentant (Matthew 18:21-22).
- You want what's best for the one who hates your guts (Matthew 5:43-44).
- You feed the hungry, shelter the homeless, and clothe the shabbily dressed just because they need it (Matthew 25:31-40).
- You welcome strangers as friends you want to make, especially if they seem a little odd to you (Matthew 25:35).

This kind of change in our spiritual posture and our real-time response to others is a tall order. Some among the fledgling Christian community in Corinth, for instance, were having a difficult time buying the idea of the resurrection. I suspect that they struggled as much or more with the possibility of becoming such different people on earth as they did with the prospect of life after death. I can't really blame them. Just look at the contrast between the way in which many of us habitually navigate the world and the example Jesus gives us to follow! Such a transformation may seem impossible, like changing stone into water. Had Jesus merely outlined a course of moral and spiritual self-improvement that any of us should be able to achieve if we tried hard enough, then we would have little cause for hope. But instead, Jesus taught us that God's love for us—and our active reception of and response to that love—shapes us into our true selves. That's the message I hear in the mysterious story of the Transfiguration.

You and Me and Transfiguration

Peter, James, and John were on a day trip with Jesus, praying on a mountaintop. Here's how Luke describes what happens next: "The appearance of [Jesus's] face changed, and his clothes became dazzling white.... They saw his glory" (Luke 9:29, 32). They saw the divinity of Jesus shining through his humanity and his humanity glowing with his divinity. The sight of the Transfiguration stirred within them an awareness of how God's love was changing them from within—a change that will come to completion for them, and for all of humanity, in the final resurrection. Jesus redeems us by transforming us into who we were meant to be from the very beginning. Let me explain how this works in three interwoven concepts.

Here's the first concept: *God sustains all things.* Franciscan theologian Bonaventure, writing in the thirteenth century, reminded us that every creature came into being as a result of an expenditure of divine energy. So everything—rocks and salamanders and red giant stars—bears the

Maker's mark. Bonaventure actually said that created things have vestiges or footprints of the Maker. But I invite you to consider this in a slightly different way. Think about glow-in-the-dark toys. They contain a substance called phosphor that absorbs light from another source and then gradually emits that light over time. By comparison, Bonaventure's point is that every created thing gives off a sort of afterglow of the divine energy, a glow that points back to the Creator. However, this analogy breaks down in an important way. Glow-in-the-dark toys stop glowing eventually. Phosphorescent balls or plastic stars that you stick on your ceiling grow dim after a while. When these things sit in a drawer, cabinet, or dark room for ages without coming into contact with a light, they still exist but just won't glow. However, time does not diminish the Creator's glow within created beings because in each instant, God is actively sustaining everything that is. If God were not expending energy to keep something in existence, it would recede into nothingness!

Here's the second concept: *God created everything for relationship.* As we've discussed previously, God created everything out of nothing, but God did not create the universe just to walk away from it or to observe it from a distance. God created everything that is for relationship. And God's first thought in this whole creation business was none other than Jesus: "In the beginning was the Word, and the Word was with God, and the Word was God" (John 1:1). God created everything by and for Christ. Some would say that's not quite right, that Jesus came along because of sin or that God became a human to save us from Adam's (and everybody else's) disobedience. In other words, no sin, no Jesus. But Christ has been involved in the world from the beginning, and when we recall that God's purpose in creation is relationship, we see that, in the Incarnation, God actually becomes a human being and remains God at the same time. Jesus is both divine and human. One being. Two completely different natures. You can't get any closer than that.

Now, let's consider the third concept: *We participate in the divine life through Jesus.* Jesus is unique. No other human being will be divine in that sense. However, the Eastern Orthodox Churches give us the concept of *theosis* or "divinization," which means that Jesus shares our humanity so we can participate in the divine life. Through the Incarnation, God makes humanity what it was always intended to be: the image of God, or to echo Bonaventure, the afterglow of God. God the Holy Spirit thoroughly inhabits us and shines through us to illuminate the world. That is our divinely intended destiny. It's where, with God's help, we are heading. We are being transformed. We just haven't arrived yet. Jesus shows us that we are our true selves when we are most human, and we are most human when we are the image of God, when we love what God loves. This is our calling, and to fulfill it, we must understand what God loves.

6

LOVING WHAT GOD LOVES

If you find that what you do each day seems to have no link
to any higher purpose, you probably want to rethink
what you're doing.
—Ronald Heifetz, *The Practice of Adaptive Leadership*

Much of the literary world blinked uncomprehendingly when the Nobel Committee first announced the winner of the 2016 prize for literature: Bob Dylan. Yes, *that* Bob Dylan: the folk singer, the rock star, the countercultural hippie poet with a marginal singing voice. In some circles, the stunned silence morphed into contempt and even outrage. Placing Dylan on a list that includes the likes of Doris Lessing, Gabriel García Márquez, Toni Morrison, and Saul Bellow was more than preposterous. It was insulting. For many, the prestige of the Nobel Prize for Literature would be forever diminished.

Personally, Dylan's Nobel honor put a smile on my face. I'm a Dylan fan, especially early Dylan. "Blowin' in the Wind" and "The Times They Are a-Changin'" appealed to me when I was younger and, I think, speak truth to us now. As a rule, the work he produced during his brief Christian phase (1979–1981) did not speak to me. However, there is one big exception. It's a song called "Gotta Serve Somebody."[1] In its refrain—"you're gonna have to serve somebody"—Dylan makes the point that in everything we do, whether momentous or ordinary, we will either love what God loves or not. We may do this deliberately or without much reflection. But still, we will "have to serve somebody." Jesus's teachings inspired these lyrics. But they could just as easily have come from the Hebrew Scriptures with which the young Jewish boy Robert Zimmerman—Bob Dylan—would have been familiar. Dylan joins both Jesus and the prophets in teaching us that what we love matters.

What We Love Matters

In his farewell speech to the tribes of Israel, Moses's successor, Joshua, said this: "Now if you are unwilling to serve the LORD, choose this day whom you will serve, whether the gods your ancestors served in the region beyond the River or the gods of the Amorites in whose land you are living" (Joshua 24:15). To put it simply, you're gonna have to serve somebody. Our actions embody a deep commitment, a devotion, to something or someone. Whether we realize it or not, whether we name it this way or not, something or someone becomes our god. By "god" I'm referring to whatever it is that we as individuals and communities believe will give our lives meaning, whatever will make our lives matter and make our lives significant. Even if we make no conscious decision on the matter, our habitual actions, the patterns of our lives reveal what god we are worshiping, to what we are entrusting our very beings.

Some of us chase celebrity. Others of us pursue wealth, power, social status, or just more stuff. We may neglect our families, health, or integrity in order to get applause, exercise control, or accumulate possessions. We can so devote ourselves to control, fame, and material assets that they function as our gods. Pursuit of them shapes the actions we choose, the relationships we form, the values we inhabit, the thoughts we think about ourselves, and the way we treat other people. This is what Richard Rohr calls serving the three P's: power, possessions, and prestige. However we label or categorize them, the Bible refers to these small "g" gods as idols.

But here's the catch: we're gonna have to serve somebody, and we can end up serving somebody who isn't worth serving. These small "g" gods offer what they cannot deliver: to satisfy our deepest longings for the infinite and the eternal. We don't want our lives to matter for a mere fifteen minutes and then be forgotten in the fog of history. We want our loves, our losses, our struggles, and our victories to have meant something—and to mean something forever.

Applause fades. You can't take your stock portfolio with you beyond the grave. Every athletic record gets broken. Every president, world champion, and Nobel Laureate is replaced by the next one. There is only one capital "G" God who delivers on the promise to make life infinitely and eternally significant: the God who made us in order to love us, the God who loves us so that we can share that love with one another. To serve this God is to commit ourselves to loving what God loves, how God loves it. And God loves the entire creation. At the dedication of the first temple, King Solomon said as much: "O Lord, God of Israel, there is no God like you in heaven above or on earth beneath, keeping covenant and steadfast love for your servants who walk before you with all their heart" (1 Kings 8:23).

We're all gonna serve somebody. The patterns of our lives will reveal who or what that is. We serve the God of Abraham and Sarah, Isaac and Rebekah, Jacob and Leah and Rachel. We serve the God of Jesus when we make the pattern of our lives the way of love. What we love matters—and how we love matters just as much.

How We Love

I love key lime pie—and carrot cake, peach cobbler, and butter pecan ice cream. Some people will say, "You don't love things. You love people. You *like* those desserts." But, honestly, I do love them. That's what we humans do. We love. We love people, animals, places, and things. For instance, I love

- gazing up at the stars from my backyard;
- smelling bread as it bakes in the oven;
- hearing frogs peeping from the bayou;

- feeling flannel against my arms on a cold day;
- kissing my dog Gracie's smooth, black forehead.

To live as a human being is to love. Our challenge is that we can love the wrong things, and we can love the right things in the wrong way.

During the penitential season of Lent, I frequently forgo dessert. My point is not to deprive myself of something I enjoy in order to earn self-denial points with God. Neither do I think dessert is a bad thing that I'll try, once again, to stop indulging in forever. Instead, I take a break from after-dinner sweets to remind myself what kind of love is appropriate to food, to other people, and to God. Love is a way of being in this world—how we live and move and have our being in space and time (Acts 17:28). The Bible tells us that loving is the defining human activity. Because we are the image of God, who is love, we actualize our humanity by loving.

A dog will be a dog. A dandelion, a dandelion. It is not in their nature to betray their doggie-ness or dandelion-ness. But we humans can be inhumane. It's not merely that we refuse to love, but we can love in the wrong way. Our enduring spiritual challenge—as the image of God on planet Earth—is to grow toward a habitual way of living that resembles divine love in the flesh. As it turns out, navigating our world in this way is how we love God with our whole heart, mind, soul, and strength (Mark 12:28-31). Jesus came to show us what this looks like and to enable us to stumble, scooch, and shuffle toward that infinite goal. The story of Jesus's temptations in the wilderness offers us a striking lesson about what and how we love at our most human (Luke 4:1-13).

After receiving John's baptism, Jesus spent forty days in the desert in preparation for his public ministry (Matthew 4:1-11). He was seeking clarity about his mission. Having fasted for the entire forty days, Jesus was understandably famished. To throw him off his game, Satan said something like this to Jesus: "No problem. Turn this heap of rocks into a nice bag of warm bagels. That'll really hit the spot." To eat when you're hungry is a good thing. Apparently, Jesus loved food. Later in his ministry his detractors would essentially call him a glutton for attending so many dinner parties. But Jesus recognized that Satan wasn't actually reminding him to get his nutrition. Instead, Satan was tempting Jesus to reduce love to consumption, to turn to things to fill his emptiness. That's why Jesus said, "One does not live by bread alone" (v. 4).

You may have heard the old saying that each of us has a God-shaped hole in our hearts. Trying to fill it with things won't work. While that's an important lesson, there's another one to be learned from this exchange between Jesus and Satan. Yes, we can sometimes love the wrong things. We can fruitlessly seek spiritual fulfillment by chasing one sensual pleasure after another or by compulsively padding our bank account. But there's another, greater danger. When we think that love amounts to filling our own emptiness, we may begin to treat other people as if they were things. We look for spouses or friends to make us feel a certain way. We grow resentful or withdraw our affections when they fail to meet our expectations.

Thing-love is always self-centered. The first and the last question is always, "What's in it for me?" There is nothing in the world wrong with loving things as things and expecting them to gratify us in the way appropriate to what they are. A loaf of bread should taste a certain way. It can fill my belly and restore my strength. But it will never give my life an abiding sense of significance. Another kind of love does this. We learn this as we follow Jesus out of the desert, onto the dusty roads of Galilee, and finally on to Jerusalem. As I have written elsewhere,

> Jesus commits himself to the healing of the world. He does whatever it takes to make the world whole. He feeds the hungry, mends the sick, and restores lunatics to sanity. He breaks bread with streetwalkers and extortionists, drug addicts and con artists. By costly example, he teaches us to forgive the unrepentant, to resist the violent with compassionate truth, and to give the thief who steals your shoes the shirt off your own back.[2]

71

By example, Jesus teaches us to love people as people. All people. Just as they are. No matter what. That kind of love is our highest and holiest aspiration. To the world, it sounds utterly implausible. But the good news is that our attempts to love do not have to be perfect in order to be holy.

Imperfect Signs of Love

During our first year of marriage, Joy and I studied at the Ruhr University in Germany. We were part of a large and diverse foreign-student population. Men and women from Iran, Iraq, Argentina, Ethiopia, and Japan majored in engineering, computer programming, literature, and philosophy. By far the largest group came from China. The office responsible for exchange students arranged regular, heavily subsidized bus trips to various parts of Germany and to other countries of the European Union. The university's aim was to encourage international understanding of and relationships with Europe. Secondarily, these trips fostered community among the foreign students.

On one of our excursions, Joy and I sat across from a young Chinese woman whom we had come to know. She asked, "How can you Christians love everyone? I love my family. I will take care of my children as they grow up and my parents as they grow old. But there are billions of people. What do you mean you love them all?" Our friend wasn't challenging us or calling our faith into question. She was genuinely curious about how we would live out a faith that makes such a bold claim: We will love everyone. No exceptions. No prerequisites. And we don't mince words about it. We sing it boldly: "They'll know we are Christians by our love, by our love."[3] Love is not one thing among many that we Christians might or might not do, like cross ourselves, kneel, raise our hands in prayer, or eat fish on Friday. To follow Jesus is to love like Jesus.

Jesus spent his earthly ministry teaching people what love is—or, more precisely, he showed us *who* love is. Again, God is love, and so Jesus is love in the flesh. What Jesus did in the flesh shows us what love is. Love is not mere affection. It is the creative, transforming power of God. John's Gospel culminates in the passion and resurrection of Jesus. But in the earlier chapters of the Gospel we read pointed lessons about the nature of love. These lessons gradually prepare us to experience the full impact of the cross and the empty tomb.

Listen to the Gospel of John's familiar opening phrase. "In the beginning was the Word" (John 1:1). The Greek words translated "in the beginning" (*en arche*) mean "at the beginning or root of things."[4] At the bottom of things. At the very core of things. Everything that is, was, or will be owes its existence to God's love. It bears repeating that God did not make a bunch of stuff and then step back to admire the handiwork. Everything depends upon God at every single instant. Each honeysuckle vine, white pelican, chubby baby, and grumpy old bulldog would tumble into the abyss of nothingness if God ceased even for a nanosecond pouring love into it. It would be like unplugging an electric appliance. The mere existence of all the animals, plants, oceans, stars, planets, and rock formations is a sign that God's love is actively present—creating, sustaining, making something happen.

Over the next eleven chapters, John recounts seven signs of God's love. The very first happens at Cana of Galilee. Along with his mom and traveling companions, Jesus shows up at a wedding where the wine runs out. At the urging of his mother, Jesus turns several huge jugs of water into wine—and I mean the really good stuff (John 2:1-11). The sign is a showing, a revelation, of God as love. God's presence transfigures things. In some ways, we've grown so accustomed to God's transforming power that we take it for granted or think of it as merely natural. Caterpillars turn into butterflies. A child grows in a woman's womb. Bare winter branches yield spring blossoms. But these are holy changes.

Other holy changes might more ably grab our attention. Parents forgive their child's murderer. Heroin addicts get sober. None of this is solely human achievement, luck of the draw, or brute natural law. This is God's love working itself out. So, when we Christians say that we will love everyone, we're admitting to an infinite desire even though we are finite beings. We yearn to have God's love work itself out through us, to be signs of a loving God in a world laced with hurt, loneliness, violence, deprivation, sorrow, and regret. God can make water into wine through us. God's love can make strangers into friends, fear into compassion, resentment into reconciliation. When the hungry are fed, the homeless are sheltered, and the sick receive treatment, God's love reveals itself.

In this life, you and I will not love perfectly. Still, our imperfections do not prevent God's love from showing through. After all, a crummy stable and a cruel cross served as signs of God's love. So, too, can our own fumbling attempts to love what God loves as God loves it. To follow Jesus is to be an imperfect sign of God's perfect love. They will know we are Christians by our messy love. And they will know we are Christians by how we graciously remind each other how to love—despite our imperfections.

So, this leads us to an important question.

What Does Your Love Look Like?

My maternal grandparents, Joseph and Marie, were joined at the hip. My mother and I spent a portion of my childhood and all of my teen years under their roof. They continued to speak German to each other and to my mother, using broken English with me. Nevertheless, I generally understood what everybody was saying in German.

Sometimes my grandfather would fall into a dark humor. He didn't fly into a rage, but he would be visibly angry, usually about money, wastefulness, or slovenliness. Most of the time his ill temper was aimed at my mother. He would stalk around the house, dusting, mopping, and grumbling to himself about what a disappointment, an irritant, or a misfit she was. My grandmother would continue silently cutting vegetables, ironing clothes, or cleaning kitchen counters. Eventually, he would turn an emotional corner and begin to simmer down a bit. Then she would say quietly, gently, and almost melodically, "*Du! Sep!*"

Du is the familiar form of "you" in German. *Sep* was the nickname that only she called her husband. Literally she was just saying, "Hey, Joe!" But I can tell you that Grandma was doing a lot more than getting his attention or starting an idle conversation. She was calling my grandfather back to himself. She wasn't telling him to calm down or lecturing him about his temper or placating him. With the voice of love, she was reminding him who he truly was. She was encouraging him to let his words and actions flow from his true self instead of letting his circumstances make him into something he didn't really want to be.

My wife, Joy, and a few of my friends love me enough to do a similar kindness for me sometimes. Life's changes and chances can rattle my cage, raise my blood pressure, or leave me despondent. It's a gift to have people who will call me back to my true self and away from merely reacting to shifting circumstances. I suspect that most of us, from time to time, need to be reminded of who we really are. But you know, I don't believe that God ever needs this reminder. Part of what makes God, well, God, is that God is always true to the divine self. "I AM WHO I AM" (Exodus 3:14); that's what God told Moses at the burning bush. So, when God is being God (which is always), God is loving, because as we've seen, love is God's eternal, unchanging essence.

God created us to be the image of God (Genesis 1:27). So, we are meant to walk in love on this planet because that's just who we are. Love is not a reaction to someone's good looks or social standing. It's not a payment for their behavior or a reward for their achievements. Love is a gift, not a transaction. Love never asks, "What's in it for me?" But we forget who we are from time to time. We distort and debase love when we use it like a currency to be earned for right thinking or right acting. Jesus came into this world as our friend to remind us who we truly are—the image of God—by showing us who God really is: *love*. Jesus did this with his life. He was born in a slum, became a refugee from a cruel king as a toddler, and died at the hands of a ruthless empire. His resurrection revealed that love's power comes from God, not from any set of earthly circumstances.

Jesus taught the lesson of love with his parables. Take, for instance, the parable of the lost sheep (Luke 15:1-7). Jesus had been hanging out with the usual disreputable crowd: Roman collaborators, winos, drug addicts, and streetwalkers. Some hyper-pious types were indignant. "Can you believe who this guy associates with? Well, if you lie down with the dogs, you'll rise with the fleas." Jesus never explains himself or defends his actions to self-righteous critics and judgmental jerks. Let's put aside what's often a customary take on this parable where Jesus justifies himself by basically saying that he came to save sinners and that everybody, even his supremely religious critics, are sinners. I mean, yeah, that's true enough. But the real punch of the parable comes with the spiritual Jiu Jitsu he does with the opening question: "Which one of you, having a hundred sheep and losing one of them, does not leave the ninety-nine in the wilderness and go after the one that is lost until he finds it?" (Luke 15:4). Let's not just blow by this question but let it flip us upside down. Instead of rushing to hear that Jesus forgives us and will pursue us when we're lost, let's really listen to the question and then get real with our answer.

Which of us would actually leave our whole herd of sheep in the middle of nowhere, surrounded by wolves and thieves, just on the off chance that we might find one that has gone missing? Well, none of us. Every one of us would do a cost-benefit analysis, at least in the background of our mind: *What's in it for me? Find the one, maybe, if it's not already wolf bait or in somebody else's stewpot. In the meantime, risk losing ninety-nine to predators of either the four- or two-legged variety. It's a no-brainer. Cut my losses.*

News flash: Jesus isn't talking about shepherding practices. He's talking about love. The question Jesus poses is this: What does your love look like?

God never cuts losses, never asks, "What's in it for me?" God loves. Period. Jesus is asking us, "What about you?" He isn't blaming us for our frailty and imperfection. He's challenging us and inviting us to grow in how we love, calling us back to our true selves—back to people who walk in love because that's just who we are. And as it turns out, love does some beautiful, unsettling, and surprising things.

PART IV

Making a Difference. Together.

Each of us has a unique part to play in the healing of the world.
—Marianne Williamson,
The Law of Divine Compensation: On Work, Money, and Miracles

7

BEING US AND BEING ME

*No man is an island, entire of itself; every man
is a piece of the continent, a part of the main.*

—John Donne, *Devotions upon Emergent Occasions, "Meditation XVII"*

She greeted the four of us with a smile of recognition and chatted with us briefly. We were regulars and had spoken to each other dozens of times. At least, she had taken scores of our drink and dinner orders. For some reason, I noticed her brown eyes that night as if for the first time. I saw the tiny laugh lines that framed them on either side and felt earthy warmth and worldly sincerity they conveyed. I kept sneaking discreet glances while she was talking to my friends. Then those eyes looked directly into mine. She asked, "What will you have?" My throat froze for an awkward moment. In a rush I was feeling—not so much thinking—something like, "I wish you would pull up a chair. Tell me who you are or what you're thinking or the kind of music you like. It's just, looking into your eyes, I believe I caught a glimpse of you. And I think you caught a glimpse of me." After an awkward moment I managed to mumble, "I'll take the nachos." That night I had no idea that this cheerful, relaxed person had been a social justice leader since high school, had graduated summa cum laude from the University of Georgia, and had walked away from a successful career teaching high school students to search for something more adventurous in life. At that moment, I only had the vague sense that we had connected.

Some time later, this woman, Joy, and I would agree to get married. No, I did not propose. We discussed it and arrived at a mutual decision. That's how we roll to this day. Now, when I look into her eyes, I am reminded of all that our eyes have seen together. Joy and I remember, albeit from different angles, the winding road that we have traveled. Our shared road has made her who she is, me who I am, and most remarkably, us who we are. It is the very idea, the living reality, that I am part of a "we" that makes my life worth living. Hope rests in part upon a sense of belonging. As we've discussed, hope involves being your true self, and your true self includes being part of a "we." Philip Newell put it this way: "We come closest to our true self when we pour ourselves out in love for one another, when we give our heart and thus the whole of our being."[1] And while I've introduced the concept of belonging by talking about my relationship with Joy, the "we" I have in mind includes more than the romantic attachments between individuals. Being your true self involves learning how to speak in first person plural, to say "we" authentically, in wider and ever more varied circles: communities, schools, congregations, movements, organizations, and the body of Christ.

The Authentic "We"

Combining the words "authentic" and "we" into a single phrase may seem odd or even contradictory. It may be especially startling to hear me suggest that the true self is a "we." I understand the resistance we have to this idea in our culture.

When Joy and I first started dating, the notion of an authentic "we" would never have occurred to me. My thinking was heavily influenced by existential philosophy, and in fact, today's popular usage of the terms "authentic" and "authenticity"—along with their opposites "inauthentic" and "inauthenticity"—bears the stamp of thinkers such as Albert Camus, Jean-Paul Sartre, and Simone de Beauvoir. From their perspective, the true self is an individual, not a "we" but an "I." As individuals, then, we are true to ourselves, or authentic, when our actions express our own inner life of intentions, desires, values, and aspirations. In fact, the existentialists emphasized the many ways in which the "we" pressures, tempts, or cons us into betraying our true selves. Friedrich Nietzsche warned about being a mindless follower of the Herd. Heidegger uncovered the insidious pressure of the *They* to conform to society's expectations. The existentialists' analysis cautions us that the power of the group can lead to a distorted form of belonging, an inauthentic "we." I readily admit that being part of an authentic "we" requires each of us to draw boundaries, clarify values, and sometimes push back against the group's common assumptions and norms.

In everyday terms, we've all strained to juggle our wants and needs with a desire to please other people, avoid rejection, and win acceptance. If you are a woman, you still contend with social pressures to assume subservient roles, to avoid assertiveness, and to accept unequal pay. If you or someone you love is part of the LGBTQ+ community, you may have stories of suppressing genuine desires for intimacy due to fear of ridicule or violence. Every day good but reticent people among us choose to remain silent when a coworker or fellow church member makes a sexist or racist remark. We've all done it. We go along to get along, despite our feelings of unease and regret, and that emotional nausea indicates that we have betrayed our true selves. We have slipped into inauthenticity in order to belong.

Writer and media commentator David Brooks contends that the existentialists and their intellectual heirs mistakenly construe each individual as a "buffered self." In their view, the true self is the inner life and the choices we freely make. Membership in a group, organization, or movement does not make us who we are. When participating in a community of people, we remain authentic individuals only by refusing to compromise or betray who we truly are on the inside. Brooks writes, "The autonomous individual is the fundamental unit of society. A community is a collection of individuals who are making their own choices about how to live."[2] In other words, for the existentialists there is no authentic "we."

They insist that, at best, we can be our true selves alongside each other, but our relationship to each other does not shape and transform who we most truly are. Brooks rejects this point of view and points to it as a predominant mindset in our culture today.

In sharp contrast to this sort of individualism, the apostle Paul teaches that the true self emerges from participation in and an abiding commitment to a web of relationships. We are who we are because of the Body to whom we belong. I'll come back to Paul's discussion of the body of Christ in a moment. But first I have to admit that my lessons in the authentic self as a "we" did not originate in an earnest study of scripture but in getting to know Joy's family of origin, the Bruces.

The Bruces are a tight-knit bunch. Joy has one brother and three sisters, and the bond among the sisters is especially close. When the sisters were still children, adults would compliment their parents on what polite, helpful girls they had raised. As was the Southern custom at the time, some of those grown-ups would then turn to one of the girls and say, "You're so cute, I just want to take you home with me." No matter which sister received the compliment, she would respond, "If you take one of us, you have to take all of us." Belonging is at the very core of each sister's true self. Mind you, these are all strong, assertive women. They do not betray themselves to win the family's acceptance. Each sister can identify her own values and feelings. Sometimes they differ about very important matters, and such differences mean that they must draw difficult boundaries and navigate conflict. Yet, through it all, they maintain a deep connection with each other that nurtures and deepens their sense of self. They are an authentic "we."

The apostle Paul characterizes the Christian community as this kind of authentic "we." He writes, "For just as the body is one and has many members, and all the members of the body, though many, are one body, so it is with Christ. For in the one Spirit we were all baptized into one body" (1 Corinthians 12:12-13). What this means is that each of us is part of an integrated, organic whole. We are not like LEGO pieces that can be attached to or removed from other pieces with no change in who we truly are. Rather, each of us is part of a body, such as a limb or an organ. To be itself, the body needs every limb and organ. Conversely, every limb and organ provide a function that makes sense only in the context of the whole body.

The hand, for instance, relies on the eye to catch a ball. If the hand is removed from the body, it can no longer do "hand-y" things. It ceases to be what we mean by hand. The now lifeless tissue can no longer grasp a fork and bring food to the mouth. Nor can it scratch an itch or wave at a friend. Each member of the body is truly what it is by virtue of belonging to and functioning within the whole. However, belonging does not require conformity. On the contrary, each member of the body must retain its difference from the others in order to participate in and sustain the life of the whole. The foot cannot be a hand. The ear cannot be an eye. Otherwise, the body would be a confused heap, not a coherent whole. Every member of the body needs every other member to be what it is as a different member. Here's how Paul puts it:

> Indeed, the body does not consist of one member but of many. If the foot would say, "Because I am not a hand, I do not belong to the body," that would not make it any less a part of the body. And if the ear would say, "Because I am not an eye, I do not belong to the body," that would not make it any less a part of the body. If the whole body were an eye, where would the hearing be? If the whole body were hearing, where would the sense of smell be? But as it is, God arranged the members in the body, each one of them, as he chose. If all were a single member, where would the body be? As it is, there are many members, yet one body.

> (1 Corinthians 12:14-20)

So, despite the individualistic emphasis of our culture, the truth is that God created us to be an authentic "we." Each of us is different, yet none of us is self-contained and self-sufficient. The well-being of each of us is connected inextricably to the well-being of everybody else—so much so, that we misuse our gifts and talents when we employ them merely for our own selfish advantage. As Paul wrote, "To each is given the manifestation of the Spirit *for the common good*" (1 Corinthians 12:7, emphasis added). When we exercise our gifts for the common good—when we love one another—God is present in those acts of love. Authentic belonging sustains and strengthens our sense that life is worth living. It actually makes us hopeful.

From time to time I still gaze into Joy's eyes, only now I see more than the vague sense of connection I glimpsed nearly four decades ago. Instead, I glimpse the life we have woven together over those years. Our eyes have loved the same people and places. We have wept, and still weep, at the absence of those who no longer walk among us. Tears of laughter, anger, and relief have filled our eyes as together we have faced life's incongruities, cruelties, and unforeseen breaks. We have shared travel to exotic places, study in foreign settings, career struggles, financial hardships, and the birth and growth of children. We have held our breath through our daughter's heart surgery, celebrated our children's graduations, and taken one agonizing day at a time during our oldest son's deployment to a war zone. We belong to each other. If you take one of us, you have to take both of us. To put it simply, we love each other.

Film and television frequently portray love as two becoming one. While that is true enough, it remains incomplete. Love at its deepest level always involves a third. I don't mean literally just one more person; I mean that our love is always expanding and incorporating an Other. When it comes to love, there's always room for more. Joy and I love each other, certainly. But our love matured not merely by getting to know each other better and differentiating ourselves with effort, grace, and patience; our love also grew in our shared love for other things and other people.

Joy and I share a love of hymns, well-prepared meals, travel to new places, and walking and talking in the woods. This common appreciation deepens our relationship, but the love grows exponentially with a third who can love in response. Since we're parents, you might expect me to draw on experiences with our children as examples. I could certainly do that, but for simplicity's sake, I want to draw on our relationship with our dog, Gracie. We rescued Gracie from a local shelter when she was ten weeks old, and she has been our constant companion ever since. The depth of my affection for Gracie has surprised me. Joy says the same. Recently I watched Gracie lay her head on Joy's lap as Joy gently stroked her head and back. I not only saw their love for each other but also actually felt delight in their love for each other. I loved them in their mutual affection. Two became three.

Now that our daughter and two sons are adults, Joy and I are hearing their perceptions and versions of the family story. The "we" is stretching and expanding as a result. Growth is not always comfortable. Each of us tells the story of us, and the truth of who we are occurs in those intersecting stories. The truth of "we" emerges from the lips of multiple narrators. That's what it means to live in community. Sometimes our stories conflict. Sometimes they amplify or complete each other. But always they reveal the full picture. It's only when our stories are the same with no variations and no contradictions that we should suspect coercion, collusion, and mendacity.

We see the authentic "we" not only in the apostle Paul's writings but also in the nature of God. The Bible tells us that God is love expressed in community. The church gives us language for this, teaching us that God is triune—one in three and three in one. The Holy One *is* a community: three persons perpetually and eternally loving each other. The Bible also says that God created humans in the divine image, which means that we are what and who we are in community. Our true self derives from our participation in an authentic "we," a "we" formed and sustained by enduring bonds of love. But it is crucial to be honest with ourselves about this, acknowledging that maintaining deep bonds of affection among a number of different individuals is a challenge. Sometimes some of us want what we want, and others compete with us, get in our way, or keep warning us about the train wreck we're about to have. Sometimes, we just don't feel like loving.

Think, Feel, Love

One simple phrase explains why we eat unhealthy foods, skip the gym, refuse to forgive, resist apologizing, avoid admitting when we're wrong, and don't ask for directions when we're lost: "I don't feel like it." We know better. Studies show, experts agree, the Bible teaches, and common sense tells us what would make for a fit body, a tranquil mind, and harmonious relationships. Yet, to paraphrase Paul in Romans 7:15, we don't do the thing we keep telling ourselves we want to do—or, at least, the thing we ought to do. The reverse is true, too. We do the very thing we hate. I do, in fact, eat the fourth giant cookie, blurt out something snarky when I'm offended, or binge-watch five episodes of *The Blacklist* instead of starting an overdue project. Why? Because, "I feel like it." And, yes, I know better. At least Paul knew how I feel afterward (Romans 7:24). There's some comfort in that.

It's almost as if we are of two minds—and as a matter of fact, that's essentially what we are. As the writer Mark Manson puts it, human consciousness is like a car with two passengers: the Thinking Brain and the Feeling Brain. The Thinking Brain is orderly and sensible. It sees the big picture, considers consequences, and plans for the long term. The Thinking Brain is a little slow and ponderous. Left all on its own, the Thinking Brain will endlessly compute possible scenarios and generate plausible strategies for dealing with them. Thinking alone will never move us anywhere. We need the Feeling Brain to propel us into action. The Feeling Brain reacts at the speed of light to what's right in front of it and gets us moving. However, for the Feeling Brain, there is no tomorrow. It is focused narrowly on the present moment and makes no provision for what will happen down the road. Without the input of thought, the Feeling Brain can push us to rash, destructive, and self-destructive behavior. Just as the Thinking Brain needs feelings for motivation, the Feeling Brain needs thoughts to provide guidance. In the healthy, balanced soul, the Thinking Brain and the Feeling Brain work together as a team. The challenge we all face is that both of these passengers (the Thinking Brain and the Feeling Brain) often insist that they should be in the driver's seat.[3]

Ancient philosophers and church leaders were horrified when they saw what can happen when you lock the "Thinking Brain" in the trunk of the car and let an unhinged "Feeling Brain" get behind the wheel. Think about Roman emperors Caligula or Nero. They overreacted. In a manner of speaking, they issued a driver's license to the Thinking Brain and stuffed the Feeling Brain kicking and screaming into a toddler's car seat. There are Christian traditions to this day that insist we should know the rules and force our emotions to walk the line. Maybe you've seen this bumper sticker: *The Bible says it, I believe it, that settles it.* Another bumper sticker complements it: *When all else fails, read the instructions.* Honestly, I do not think the Bible lends itself to a plain reading. It's a nuanced library of books that yields a variety of interpretations to equally faithful people. Scripture is way more than an instruction manual. But even if I believed that these bumper stickers spoke some serious truth, there would remain one giant problem: the human psyche. Sometimes you just don't feel like doing what the instructions say. This is actually a huge problem because, as psychologists have learned, without the Feeling Brain, the car will not move. And following Jesus requires us to move.

I'm not a follow-the-instructions kind of guy. I'm a follow-the-example-of-Jesus kind of guy, you know, walk the way of love. But I have to tell you, this doesn't really get me off the hook because, well, sometimes I don't feel like it. Jesus says, "Love your enemies" (Luke 6:27). Do I really have to go any further? Well, I will anyway. Turn the other cheek, he says. Give the shirt off your back and your last dime to every beggar you meet. Don't even protect your stuff from thieves (Luke 6:28-31). Act like you want *everybody* to be a part of your community. Jesus wants us to treat everyone as part of the "we," even if we think they'll make a stinking mess of the place.

Gee, Jesus, that sounds awfully saintly. All very loving. But when somebody spits in my eye, bullies my kid, swipes my iPad, or talks trash about me behind my back, I don't feel like it. As it turns out, Jesus knows this about me and you and pretty much everybody. He's asking a lot. He's asking us to grow into the image of God—into our true selves. He's asking us to make our lives the way of love. And he realizes that this won't happen all at once. There's a learning curve, not only for our heads but for our hearts as well. Sometimes we will have to emulate Jesus's behavior before our emotions have caught up with him. This takes courage and patience. Here's what he suggests: Fake it 'til you make it. Do loving things even when your heart's not completely in it yet. As some contemporary therapists tell us, our actions can influence and transform our emotions.[4] So, try doing the loving thing no matter what. Expect to fall flat on your face, but count on Jesus to pick you up, dust you off, and hold you by the elbow as you limp along for the next few miles. This is the kind of love—a sometimes hard-won love—that can move wary strangers toward seeing each other as the beloved children of God.

God's Children

When Joy and I went looking for a dog, we wanted an adult, not a puppy. We had in mind an abandoned or discarded pet less likely to be welcomed into someone else's home. But that's not how things worked out. Ten-week-old Gracie did not jostle with the rest of the pack to get our attention and affection. Instead, she lay off to one side, curled in a ball, alone and sleeping. She seemed to have given up, having been passed over again and again for cuter, more enthusiastic dogs. While she was still sleeping, I scooped her up and held her for a bit. Then Joy cuddled her against her chest. That's how this little black, mixed-breed dog joined our family. We loved her from the start.

Out of curiosity we bought a doggie-DNA kit to learn about her genetic makeup. The results told us that she's a mix of retriever, hound, terrier, and cattle dog, though we've never been interested in establishing her pedigree. For us, she's just one of a kind. She's Gracie. By contrast, pedigree is important to people wanting to breed and show dogs. The bloodline has to be pure. If there's a bulldog hidden somewhere in a sheltie's lineage, then it's nothing more than a mixed breed or mutt. It will never be allowed to compete in the Westminster Kennel Club Dog Show. Of course, bloodline is an antiquated way to express what we now know as DNA. But once upon a time, we talked about dog breeds in terms of the kind of blood running through their veins, and some blood was considered to be better than others.

As ghastly as it is to admit, throughout history we have thought in similar terms about our fellow human beings, valuing some more than others based on their bloodline. Here are two especially stark examples from the previous century. In 1935, the Nazi Party established the Nuremberg Laws. These statutes stripped anyone with a sufficient amount of Jewish blood of all rights as a citizen. You were a Jew if your bloodline included three or four Jewish grandparents. Eventually, this led to the gas chambers and the near extermination of the Jews of Europe. Closer to home, some of our states passed legislation using blood to define race. The notorious one-drop rule held that even a single drop of "Negro blood"—even one black ancestor— sufficed to classify someone as "colored" and hence ineligible to vote. With the Civil Rights Act of 1964, voting restrictions based on race were abolished, but racism did not disappear. For instance, in my own state of Louisiana, the legislature passed a law in 1970 decreeing that a person can be considered white if they have 1/32 or less of "Negro blood." That law was repealed in 1983 in part because wide, unfavorable media attention had been given to a court case originated in Sulphur, Louisiana. A woman who self-identified as "white" objected to having "colored" on her birth certificate.[5] To her, being "white" was at least socially preferable to being "colored." "Bloodline thinking" is a way to justify the view that some people are better than others. This way of thinking arrived with the first settlers on the shores of North America and has been with us ever since in one form or another. It extends beyond the personal prejudice and hateful ignorance of individuals to involve laws and common business practices that have privileged white people and put black and brown people at a disadvantage.

As it turns out, Jesus confronted bloodline thinking in his own day. Luke tells us that, on his way to Jerusalem, Jesus passed through a village along the border of Galilee and Samaria and, at the outskirts of town, healed ten lepers. Adhering to scriptural protocol, he sent all of them to the priest, the only one who had the authority to pronounce them clean and restore them from outcast status to normal life among their neighbors. When one of those lepers raced back to thank Jesus, he basically said, "Why look! Only one of the people I just healed took the time to thank me. And what do you know! It's a Samaritan" (Luke 17:11-19).

Although we can reasonably draw a lesson about gratitude from this story (after all, Jesus himself took the man's gratefulness as an expression of his robust, exemplary faith), Jesus was not emphasizing the healed leper's gratitude as much as he was the man's ethnic identity. The healed leper was a Samaritan, and Samaritans were considered half-breeds. After Israel had been divided into two separate Kingdoms (Israel in the north and Judah in the south) and the Assyrians had conquered the Northern Kingdom, many of its citizens were scattered, and intermarriage with other ethnic groups became common. As a result, many residents of Judah looked askance at the bloodline of the Samaritans, considering them not to be the true children of God. So when Jesus praised the Samaritan's faith and virtue, the disciples would have heard Jesus affirming who he was. Perhaps the unspoken message was something like this:

> Each of us is one of a kind, yet we all belong to one bloodline.
> God's love makes you a true child of God—not where you
> grew up, not who your parents were, not the language you
> speak or the color of your skin. God loves everybody. We're all
> God's children, members of God's family. We all belong.

I believe the strength of our hope grows with our ability to say, "If you take one of us, you have to take all of us." The relentless power of this love can make a decisive difference in this troubled, aching world.

8

HOW LOVE MAKES A DIFFERENCE

We can be heroes, just for one day.

—David Bowie, "Heroes"

My friend Ira once said something like this to me: "You Christians are lucky. You believe that you'll live forever, so you don't have to worry about being forgotten. I don't believe in an afterlife. So I have to accomplish something in this life, or nobody is going to remember me. My life won't have mattered. I might just as well have never existed." What I heard Ira saying is that he felt that his life was worth living only if he made a difference in this world, and not just any difference, but a difference that would endure beyond his death.

As a college professor and scholar, Ira was thinking about making lasting contributions in his area of expertise. He had never published a book or an article recognized by his academic peers as significant in their field. With retirement in sight, Ira was beginning to wonder if his life might have been futile. The universe as he understood it would not remember his name. There would be no memorial reminding successive generations that he had walked the same earth and that the place would not be the same had he not been here.

Ira was being very vulnerable with me about an emotionally trying place in his life. So, I listened. It wasn't the moment to explain to him that

93

Christians think of eternal life as much more than merely living forever. Actually, as we've discussed, eternal life is a way of being that begins right here on planet Earth. It's what Episcopal Presiding Bishop Michael Curry calls a way of love. As we open ourselves more and more to God's loving presence among us, we recognize ourselves more clearly as the beloved. Then we lean into our true selves as God's beloved by pouring that love out to the world we inhabit.

As we've seen, love is not a mere emotion. Love is the power to heal, to nurture, to resist, and to liberate. When we love, we are most fully ourselves; when we are ourselves, we make a difference. Our lives feel worth living. We have hope. What sometimes gnaws away at our hope is that the differences we make can seem so small, insignificant, and fleeting. The truth is that, even (and perhaps especially) in our humble acts of love, we serve as God's agents of radical liberation.

Radical Liberation

My mother used to say, "You have to take the bad with the good." When I was disappointed, flabbergasted, outraged, or frustrated, those words never failed to infuriate me. What I heard her saying was, "Calm down." In retrospect, I've come to recognize that she probably meant to convey a lesson about life I wasn't yet prepared to receive. She was trying to help me see what it means to persist in being a person committed to nurture and healing in a world bent on breaking hearts, minds, and bodies.

The only story my mother ever told me about Mauthausen Concentration Camp was her liberation. Viciously beaten and left for dead by a German officer, my mother woke to find her wounds being tended by a GI. Her captors had fled ahead of their advancing enemy. In a movie or novel, this episode might serve as the happy ending. She was free at last, and that was that. The strife was o'er, the battle won. She lived happily ever after. Only, she didn't. In her personal life, she endured—and eventually escaped—an abusive husband. Two of her children, my brother, Joseph, and my sister, Marie, preceded her in death. The question for her was always, "Who will I be in response to this world?" She had been liberated from that dreadful camp, but she still lived in a world that devised such camps. She had been liberated into a world that still needed liberating. She would have to take the bad with the good, to respond to the bad with the good, to be a force of liberation especially when and where the forces of captivity redoubled their efforts. As the apostle Paul put it, "Do not be overcome by evil, but overcome evil with good" (Romans 12:21).

Speaking to his friends, Jesus said something analogous to this just after he emerged from the tomb. They were now people of the Resurrection in a world that still crucified people, and this is what he had to say to them: "If you forgive the sins of any, they are forgiven them; if you retain the sins of any, they are retained" (John 20:23). We will be the people who heal and nurture, or we will perpetuate a world that returns violence for violence and wound for wound. We cannot liberate this world by putting people in concentration camps—even the very people who would still build concentration camps.

To be honest, sometimes I get weary and discouraged with this healing, nurturing work to which Jesus calls us. I'm a fan of closure and happy endings. It's tempting to believe that we could just eradicate the bad so that we're left only with the good. These feelings grow especially acute when it seems that violence, prejudice, greed, and selfishness are on the rise. But Jesus warns us that this is a dangerous, ultimately self-serving, and destructive illusion. In one parable he puts it like this: Some weeds popped up in a wheat field. Workers wanted to pull up the weeds, but the landowner stopped them, saying that if you try to yank out the weeds you'll just pull up the wheat along with them (Matthew 13:24-30). That's the Kingdom as we now know it. You have to take the bad with the good. But you do not have to resign yourself to the bad.

In another parable Jesus tells us that the kingdom of heaven is like yeast (Matthew 13:33). In quantity, the yeast is negligible compared to the lump of dough, but without the yeast, the entire mass would collapse in on itself. The yeast is present precisely for the sake of the whole. You have to take the bad with the good. Eventually, the good will make something out of even the bad. I don't mean to suggest any false equivalencies here. There are captives and captors in this world, forces of love and forces of hate. There are those who pursue the common good, recognizing that to rob any person of dignity diminishes the dignity of every human being. And there are those who seek their own comforts, advantages, privileges at the cost of others' deprivation and misery. Yet our intention to liberate not only the captives from their captors but also the captors from themselves ushers into this world the transforming force of love. When we pay attention, we can see love's transforming effect in our ordinary routines.

Transforming Love Is Resilient Love

Early on most mornings my wife, Joy, our dog, Gracie, and I leave our neighborhood by foot to walk among the longleaf pines of the Kisatchie National Forest. Onyx lives at the next-to-last house before we hit the winding, two-lane road that takes us into the woods. Our initial encounters with Onyx were unpleasant. We heard him before we saw him. His rapid, high-pitched bark warned us that we were not welcome. A black and dirty-gray mass of wiry, matted hair darted toward us from the dark. With his short legs, he ran mad circles around us, yapping and swooping in to nip at our heels until we had passed beyond his yard. On each successive walk, we set off the Onyx alarm.

We weren't intimidated by Onyx. His untamed coat makes it hard to assess his size accurately, but I estimate that he weighs, at most, fifteen pounds. Still, his frantic barking and nipping put a serious dent in what was supposed to be a contemplative walk to welcome the break of day.

Initially, we ignored him and hoped he would get used to us, or at the very least get bored with barking at the same people over and over. No luck.

Next, I used an "alpha" voice and issued common commands to get Onyx to back off:

"Sit."

"Stay."

"Switch to decaf."

Nothing but bark, dash, and nip.

Things began to change when we learned the dog's name. One morning his human scurried out of his house, still in his pajamas, and scooped the dog up.

"Sorry," he said. "He's a rescue." We chatted a moment, and I asked my neighbor what he called his dog.

"Onyx," he said.

Beginning the next morning, I greeted our little antagonist with a cheerful, "Good morning, Onyx! You're a good boy!" In gentle, soothing tones I would say, "It's just us. I'm glad to see you." Bark. Dash. Nip. Day after day, nothing changed. Joy and Gracie rolled their eyes—at me, not Onyx. And then one morning, Onyx trotted to within a few yards, acknowledged us with a glance, walked parallel with us for a minute or so, and found something more interesting to do. That became his new pattern. I interpret his behavior to mean that our presence no longer threatens him. He doesn't have to protect his turf. He doesn't fear that we'll harm him or anyone in his human pack.

This is a sweet story, and you might expect me to stop there and turn to musing about love's power to change our world. While I believe that love— and only love—can change the deep rhythms of this world, I'm aware that such love can come at a cost. Love is risky, because powerful and often violent forces prefer this world the way it is. They like it just fine, because they are on top, and these forces will do whatever is necessary to retain their positions of privilege, power, status, and wealth.

Just as I was beginning to feel like the patron saint of dog whispering—a regular icon of the transformational power of love—I imagined how I would have responded to Onyx had he been a Rottweiler, or maybe a pit bull. These large, muscular breeds have been unfairly stereotyped as aggressive and dangerous. But in fact, they can be remarkably loving. Still, we've all heard stories of such dogs being abused, and the truth is that if a powerful, eighty-pound dog charged at me from out of the dark, I would feel threatened, and I might react aggressively myself. That's a problem.

I follow Jesus, and Jesus walked the way of love because he believed that God would change everything through his unflinching loving. Jesus didn't love only when it was easy, convenient, or rewarding. He loved all the way to the cross. He loved from the cross itself. He loved even those who nailed him to it. What's hard for us to get our heads around is that Jesus teaches us to love even though he knows full well that our love will not always result in moonbeams and rainbows. He was realistic. The kind of love Jesus shows threatens people. It makes them anxious, because it changes the world. The hungry are fed, the blind see, and the lame are empowered to take up their own mats and hit the road. Jesus forgives the unrepentant and loves his most lethal enemies. His way of loving turns the world upside down.

No wonder some rogue Pharisees once tried to shut Jesus down with threats that Herod was gunning for him (Luke 13:31-35). Most Pharisees were deeply faithful, forerunners of today's rabbis. But this bunch were phonies. They had cozied up to Herod, who was himself a corrupt Israelite stooge for the Roman Empire. These charlatans were out to get a little taste of privilege for themselves. So, in cahoots with Herod, they used their habitual strategy to protect their status. They threatened violence in order to run Jesus off and shut him up. In case they couldn't intimidate Jesus into silence, they still might have succeeded in goading him into an angry, aggressive reaction. Getting Jesus to use violence would have made him look like just one more of them, and their world would remain safely intact.

But Jesus confounded them with resilient love. Here's the message he sent back to Herod: "I am casting out demons and performing cures today and tomorrow, and on the third day I finish my work" (v. 32). In other words,

"Do what you have to do, but I'm going to keep on loving. I'm going to make people whole and heal the world the only way that works, through love." Jesus understood where all of this was heading: the cross. Eventually, the Romans would execute him. He threatened them not as a rival empire would, but as a power that dismantles every empire, a power that will make the last first and the first last, a power that makes everyone equal as the beloved children of God. That power is love. To paraphrase Martin Luther King, Jr.,[1] you need light to overcome darkness, and only love overcomes hate. Darkness illuminates nothing, and adding hate to hate just results in more hate.

Jesus could be resilient, he could keep loving, even in the face of suffering and death, because he knew that the love flowing through him originated in God. That love will overcome the very worst that any empire can throw at it—even death itself. Jesus calls you and me to follow his example of resilient love, choosing to love when it seems fruitless or even painful. He's not promising us that love will right every injustice, heal every wound, and dry every tear in our lifetime. Neither is he suggesting that we will change the world ourselves with mere human wit, ingenuity, and power. Instead, he shows us what it looks like to live in a world that is at once breathtakingly lovely and shockingly brutal with a bone-deep trust in God's love, believing that it is decisively restoring and renewing the entire creation. This kind of Jesus-like trust in God's love translates into the many ways in which we love our neighbor every day—into compassion, resistance, gentleness, and resilience. Each of us is drawn to participate in this divine love wherever we are, even when it may seem as if the forces of selfishness and violence are having the last word. Especially then.

The Tattooist of Auschwitz

Most of us associate the word "Auschwitz" with unspeakable cruelty and debilitating misery, and well we should. As such, I initially assumed that Heather Morris's novel *The Tattooist of Auschwitz*, which is based on the true story of Lale Sokolov,[2] would be the account of either a callous Nazi bureaucrat or a sadistic collaborator willingly adding to the misery of his fellow captives through his services as the concentration camp tattooist. I could not have been more mistaken.

The tale of Lale Sokolov teaches us that love makes life worth living in even the most horrific situations. It illustrates what Paul teaches us about love. Without love, we are "a noisy gong or a clanging cymbal" (1 Corinthians 13:1). Without love, our lives are pointless—one numbing thing after another, a seemingly endless, exhausting sequence of events. By contrast, our love for the other gives us a why, the reason we take the next step in even the most harrowing circumstances. As Paul puts it, love "bears all things, believes all things, hopes all things, endures all things" (1 Corinthians 13:7). This is what we can see in Lale Sokolov's story.

Lale was born in Slovakia in 1916. After the Nazi occupation of 1938, Jews were eventually forbidden to work. The Nazis seized Jewish shops and factories, but mass deportations did not begin right away. For a time, the horrors of the Holocaust remained unknown to locals. Nazi occupiers demanded that each family surrender one adult to work for the Germans. If a family failed to comply, every member would be arrested. Lale volunteered for the love of his family. He sought to trade his labor for their lives.

In 1942, Lale found himself in a cattle car rolling toward an unknown destination. After arriving in what turned out to be Auschwitz, he briefly worked construction until he contracted typhoid. As a result of his illness, the Nazis shifted his duties to the admissions section of the camp, perhaps because of his knowledge of languages. There he was assigned the job of assistant tattooist and, finally, chief tattooist.

Tattooing serial numbers on the arms of men was emotionally difficult, but tattooing women nearly undid him. One day, he looked into the eyes of a young woman as he held her arm, and he fell in love with her. He learned that her name was Gita and that she lived in the women's sub-camp. Because he was chief tattooist, Lale's quarters and rations were a little better than those in the other sections of the camp. He set aside his extra rations and secreted them to Gita, her friends, his old block mates, and prisoners in the most desperate need.

Even in this ghastliest and most perilous of neighborhoods, love of neighbor continued to define Lale's daily life. The threat of torture and death hovered over him constantly. From one perspective, you might say that he risked his life to show this kind of love, but I don't think this is accurate. To me, it seems he lived because he loved. Certainly a Nazi bullet or the gas chamber would have terminated Lale's biological existence whether he loved or not. But to pursue his own survival in disregard of his neighbor, to yield to the temptation of self-centeredness, would have led to his spiritual death. He would have condemned himself to a hollow existence, to being a noisy gong or clanging cymbal.

Before the Soviet Army liberated Auschwitz, the Nazis shipped Gita out. Eventually, Lale left the camp and returned home. Soon, he set out to find Gita amid the chaos of millions of liberated survivors. Driving a horse and cart, he traveled to Bratislava. On the road to the Red Cross station serving refugees, a woman suddenly stepped in front of his cart. Gita had found Lale. Eventually Lale and Gita married and immigrated to Australia. There, Lale set up his own business, and Gita gave birth to their only son.

Lale and Gita's remarkably happy ending was not a divinely bestowed reward for their loving behavior. Many prisoners who loved just as selflessly perished before the Allies liberated the camps. Their loving actions did not magically guarantee anyone's survival. Their compassion did not prevent starvation, disease, torture, and gas from snatching the breath of millions. However, with each breath they took, those who loved their starving, ragged, weary neighbors did more than merely survive. They participated in God's own life.

If God is love, as we have said, then when we love, it is because God is flowing into our lives. God's loving presence within us transforms our self-centered impulse toward personal survival into others-directed

LOOKING FOR GOD IN MESSY PLACES

compassion. God pours this love into us so that it will overflow into the world around us. God's love for us becomes a life-giving, liberating love for our neighbor. By loving, we act as midwives of God's own love on our planet. That, I think, is one of the lessons of the birth of Jesus.

Christ's Midwives

God was born. Just let that sink in for a minute. The architect of galaxies and protons, the maker of hard iron and tender flesh, the infinite, all-powerful source from which all things come to be and upon which the entire cosmos depends, became a human. And God came into this world just like the rest of us did. A woman gave birth to him. Jesus grew day by day in the dark warmth of Mary's womb. He bumped along with her every stride, slumbering and waking to the rhythms of her heart, nudging her from within with tiny feet and sharp little elbows when his cozy home started feeling cramped. And then, on one specific day in history, in a particular place on this very planet, God was born.

How weird is that! God brought all of time and space into being from nothingness. That same God was born in an obscure corner of a tiny blue speck floating in the midst of a universe so vast that we measure its distances in light years. Theologians have been wrestling with how this could be for centuries. Among other things, that's how we got the doctrine of the Trinity. And those theologians might remind us that it was the Son—the second person of the Trinity—who became incarnate. We Christians of a liturgical stripe say this routinely when we recite the Nicene Creed:

> We believe in one Lord, Jesus Christ,
> the only Son of God,
> eternally begotten of the Father,
> God from God, Light from Light,
> true God from true God,
> begotten, not made,
> of one Being with the Father.[3]

By contrast, Luke takes our breath away simply with the story of a baby being born, a human baby like any baby. Only, not just any baby. This baby was also Emmanuel, "God with us," the long-awaited Messiah. Listen to Luke's implied punchline one more time: God was born. And because God was born, nothing would ever be the same again. You see, God wasn't born just for the heck of it. God was born for us. That's what the angels told a group of shepherds: "To you is born this day in the city of David a Savior, who is the Messiah, the Lord. This will be a sign for you: you will find a child wrapped in bands of cloth and lying in a manger" (Luke 2:11-12).

Mary and Joseph had traveled from Nazareth to Joseph's ancestral home, Bethlehem, by order of Caesar Augustus. The Emperor wanted to count all of his subjects. Like most people I know, I used to think that the expectant mother and her husband had traveled alone to Bethlehem. Once there, the inns were full, so she gave birth in a barn. However, writer Sarah Bessey offers a different perspective.[4] Given the customs of the day, it's likely that Joseph and Mary had traveled with a large group of family members, and once they got to their destination, they weren't turned away by a desk clerk from what we might think of as a hotel.

In those days, travelers stayed in the guest rooms of local residents. This is what Luke would have meant when he referred to the inn. Joseph and Mary arrived only to find out that every guest room in every house was already occupied. So, one homeowner let them stay in the public area of his house. They stayed under that innkeeper's roof, only in what might be called the family room. In those days, people kept their livestock in that part of the house, so it may have been a bit rustic. And with all the animals as well as the host of accompanying aunts and uncles and cousins crowded into the space, everyone might have felt a bit cramped. When Mary's time came, the older, experienced women no doubt leapt into action as Jesus's midwives. God needed a midwife in order to come into this world.

If God planned to become a human from the very beginning, as we considered earlier, and Jesus came to God's mind before God created anything at all, then love was God's sole motivation for bringing everything into existence. God's deep desire is to be one with the creation, and God fulfills this desire in Jesus. As fully human and fully divine, Jesus is the ultimate expression of God's unity with humanity and, through that, with all creatures. God did not think up Jesus to deal with the unanticipated problem of sin. Nevertheless, to be one with us, God must deal with the long and painful arc of human history, which has left us wounded, lonely, grief-stricken, and burdened with regret. Violence, hatred, oppression, and suffering have shattered this world. We yearn for peace with our neighbors and tranquility in our hearts. The good news for us is that in the birth of Jesus, God has embraced us just as we are, and healing comes with that divine embrace. Eventually.

The baby Jesus was born of Mary over two thousand years ago, yet our healing remains incomplete. We are not at peace in our world or in our souls. But we need not despair. Though the baby Jesus cannot be born again, the risen Jesus can be—and *yearns* to be—born on this planet every day in you and me. We are God's midwives here on Earth every time we love. When we feed the hungry and help addicts get sober; when we encourage a child and forgive the one who broke our heart; when we hold a lonely hand, cry with a grieving friend, and laugh with an unlikely stranger, God is born. When we love, the risen Christ comes into this world.

In a way, the Christmas story is still being written. God is still being born, and we are crucial characters in the story. We are God's midwives. This is how we make a difference, together.

PART V

Faith, Hope, and Friendship with God

People who've had any genuine spiritual experience always know they don't know. They are utterly humbled before mystery. They are in awe before the abyss of it all, in wonder at eternity and depth, and a Love, which is incomprehensible to the mind.

—Richard Rohr,
"Utterly Humbled by Mystery" at NPR's *This I Believe*

9

FRIENDSHIP WITH GOD

If you believe at fifty what you believed at fifteen,
then you have not lived—or have denied the reality of your life.

—Christian Wiman, *My Bright Abyss*

The committee had scheduled my interview for seven o'clock in the evening. Three professors—one each from the English, history, and religion departments—had been speaking to doctoral students all day. Each of us had applied for a fellowship to support us financially while we were writing our dissertations at one or another foreign university. As I recall, my time slot put me at the very end of an exhaustingly long line of what I imagined had been tense intellectual interrogations. A panel of seasoned scholars would soon be grilling me about the relative importance of the contribution I sought to make in philosophy and my ability to accomplish what I proposed. Imagine the academic version of the television show *Shark Tank*.

When the time for the interview arrived, my palms were sweaty, my heart was pounding, and my mouth had gone so dry that I wasn't sure I would be able to speak. I had been anticipating a boardroom with stern examiners on one side of an imposing table and me on the other. Instead, the appointed room was a lounge furnished with couches and overstuffed chairs arranged in a circle. Three cheery, laid-back men greeted me warmly and invited me to have a seat. What was it, they wanted to know, that excited me about my research project? They listened with sincere interest, and we all engaged in amiable, lively conversation.

Broadly speaking, my dissertation asked how we understand the meaning of what people have said, written, and done, especially when those people lived in a distant historical period and in a culture different from our own. Philosophers, theologians, and biblical scholars call this field of study "hermeneutics." My thesis was that we interpret meaning by placing someone's words and actions in the context from which they arose. That sounds simple enough. But things get complicated when you realize that each of us brings our own context—our own specific social and historical set of more or less conscious assumptions and commitments—to the process of interpretation. In this way, we always bring our own limited perspective to understanding. Since our perspective evolves and shifts over time, our interpretations change. Our understanding of things is always open to correction, growth, and even radical revision.

As our conversation was coming to a close, the religion professor asked, "What led you to pursue philosophy rather than religion?"

After a pause, I answered, "I can't bring myself to approach things dogmatically."

With a nod and a smile he said, "That's what I sensed about you."

At the time it didn't occur to me that a deeply religious person could be anything but dogmatic and rigidly unquestioning about matters of faith. In retrospect, I've come to suspect that this religion professor saw that my understanding of faith was unsophisticated. He was simply too kind to correct (and to embarrass) an aspiring but inexperienced scholar. My assumption at that time was that faith required not only believing the doctrines of the church but also taking a dogmatic attitude toward them. By "dogmatic attitude," I mean an adamant refusal to question a set of received concepts and a near militant rejection of doubt about them. A dogmatic attitude insists that certain questions are closed once and for all; the institutionally-agreed-upon answers to these questions form the standard by which any other truth claims about God, human conduct, or the universe will be accepted or condemned. A dogmatic Roman Catholic would recite the catechism. A dogmatic Protestant would point to what he or she takes to be a plain reading of scripture. By contrast, philosophers like me would never stop asking questions and broadening our perspective.

With some chagrin, I now realize that what I took to be a philosophical posture in contrast to religious dogmatism actually describes the sort of authentic faith that this kindly religion professor likely lived—the kind of faith that Scripture talks about, that Jesus patterned for us, and that today I, along with countless other Christians, aspire to embody. I was right that a dogmatic attitude focuses on knowing unwavering truths about God. But what I didn't understand then, and what I want to explore in this chapter, is that authentic faith focuses on being true to a friend. As Jesus told his followers, faith is about a sincere and ever-deepening friendship with God in Christ.

Being True

Once the dishes from the Last Supper had been cleared, Jesus shared a rich, extended meditation with the disciples that commentators often call "the Farewell Discourse" (John 13–17). In part, he was preparing them to navigate the shock, fear, and profound disorientation they would feel when he was arrested, tortured, and crucified. He told them something like this: "Take heart. Don't give up. This is not the end. But it is also a beginning, a divine beginning" (adapted from John 14:1-2). They would be following Jesus in a new, more intimate, and bolder way than they had before. Previously, they had been like obedient servants, but from now on they would be friends. Jesus said, "I do not call you servants any longer, because the servant does not know what the master is doing; but I have called you friends, because I have made known to you everything that I have heard from my Father" (John 15:15). The essence of faith is friendship with God in Christ.

To get Jesus's point, we have to think about what he meant by friendship. In the era of Facebook, many of us use the word "friend" to refer to relatively superficial connections with other people who might more accurately be called "acquaintances." We know a name, a face, and some details about a person: job title, hometown, education level. Other sorts of relationships revolve around leisure activities. We might bond by duck hunting, golfing, fishing, and traveling together. Still others of us forge relationships at our jobs. We assist each other on projects, help build skills, and commiserate about life and work. Any of these relationships can involve strong affection and enduring good will, but Jesus had something deeper in mind when he called his followers "friends."

Wisdom is at the heart of the relationship that Jesus had with his friends. Jesus was divine wisdom incarnate. According to Paul, Jesus "became for us wisdom from God" (1 Corinthians 1:30). Wisdom is the art of doing the loving, God-shaped thing in all the varied, changing, and nuanced situations that life hands us. Jesus reached out in friendship to Andrew, Peter, John, and the rest from the very first. He offered to impart his wisdom to them. As we'll see in a moment, that means he offered to give himself to them. Now, he was telling them, they had begun returning that friendship. Their relationship with him had become the navigational principle for their very lives. In Jesus, wisdom personified had entered and now defined their souls. As we read in the Wisdom of Solomon, this is what made them friends of God:

> In every generation [Wisdom] passes into holy souls
> and makes them friends of God, and prophets;
> for God loves nothing so much as the person who lives with wisdom.
> (Wisdom 7:27b-28, Apocrypha)

Jesus was echoing Wisdom Literature when he said, "I am the way, and the truth, and the life" (John 14:6). When we love like him, when we devote ourselves to the well-being of others and to the healing of this world, we are braiding our lives together with his. Already on this side of the grave we begin participating in the eternal life embodied by the risen Jesus.

I recognize that not all of us read Jesus's words the same way. Some may insist on the truth of propositions inscribed in a confessional statement, a creed, or a particular view or interpretation of Scripture. Faith, as they see it, requires asserting the truth of certain ideas. I am encouraging us, however, to hear Jesus teaching us that faith is about faithfulness to a person, about being true to him as friend at all times and in all places. Jesus was clear about how to do that. He said, "I give you a new commandment, that you love one another. Just as I have loved you, you also should love one another" (John 13:34). We remain faithful to Jesus and we grow in our relationship with him when we love others like Jesus loves us.

Let me be clear. I am not suggesting that we merely observe how Jesus acted and then try our very best to mimic his behavior. If all Jesus did was give us an example to copy, then he would be just one more self-improvement guru. Instead, Jesus is inviting us to participate in his life. When we love, Christ's love—Christ himself—is welling up within us, overflowing into the world and transforming our souls in the process. That's what he was getting at when he called himself the "true vine" (John 15:1). The risen Christ abides in us, and we abide in him: "I am the vine, you are the branches. Those who abide in me and I in them bear much fruit. . . . As the Father has loved me, so I have loved you; abide in my love. If you keep my commandments, you will abide in my love" (John 15:5, 9-10). The branch draws its life from the depths of the vine. Branch and vine can be differentiated, but they are still made of the same stuff, and if the branch is torn from the vine, it withers and dies.

It follows that when Jesus says he is the way, the truth, and the life (John 14:6), he is saying that a true faith is first and foremost about fidelity, not about right thinking. In Jesus, God perpetually reaches out to us in friendship—not because of what we have done but simply because God is love. Period. That is God's faithfulness to us. Our faithfulness is always a response to the divine initiative. We say yes to Christ's offer of friendship not only with our lips but in our lives, to echo a prayer from my Episcopal tradition.[1] Loving our neighbor is how we remain faithful to the risen Christ. As Jesus puts it, "You are my friends if you do what I command you" (John 15:14). What he commands is love.

Love begins when we make ourselves vulnerable to God's love. When we drop our pretenses and lower our defenses to let Christ into the tender, shabby, ordinary life we actually live. For many of us, that can be very difficult. Initially, we might even feel the pain of being exposed.

Being Exposed

Even before noon, the high summer heat and humidity of South Georgia can be stifling. It was not unusual for me to run into several of my elementary school friends at the city pool in our tiny town. On that particular morning, I noticed that my classmate Mary was standing waist-deep at the pool's edge. I had an enormous crush on her, so my heart leapt into my throat when I noticed her stealing glances at me and quickly turning away with a shy smile. No way was I going over to talk to her. But to my surprise, she motioned our friend Roger over to her, whispered something into his ear, urged him in my direction, and watched him expectantly as he padded over to me. I prepared myself for a secret love message.

Roger sidled up to me and announced in a voice that carried across the length of the pool and maybe on to the neighboring town, "Mary told me to tell you that you've got a split in your swimming trunks." Laughing, he added, "Boy, you sure do. You're hanging completely out!"

My trunks were a carryover from the previous summer. They were too tight, and the seam in the back had given way from waistband to crotch. I was exposed. Judging from the look on Mary's face, she hadn't meant for the news to be passed along in such a public way. It was not her intention to embarrass me but to warn me and to give me a quiet exit. But embarrassed I was. To borrow a phrase from Brené Brown, I had a hurricane-force shame storm. I rushed home and, to the best of my recollection, never returned to that pool.

Many of us, maybe all of us, have things that we do not easily or readily share with others. Sometimes, people intentionally hide bad things like past wrongdoing, cruel thoughts, or evil intentions. But mostly we hold parts of ourselves in reserve for the sake of emotional self-preservation. We bear old wounds, carry tender feelings, nurture fragile dreams, and retain painful regrets. Letting someone else in on such personal matters makes us very vulnerable. We can experience intimacy this way, but we also risk rejection, ridicule, judgment, or indifference.

Imagine what it would be like for someone to see everything about you. None of your filters, none of your habitual defenses and practiced facades prevent that person from seeing you just as you are. You're exposed. Encountering the holy involves being exposed in this way; it is an experience of being seen at the most granular level, becoming aware that we are being known in all our lunacy, beauty, messiness, and fragility. I believe that all true religion and all meaningful spirituality begins in and ever returns to just such an encounter.

Theologian Karl Rahner once said that if there are to be Christians in the future at all, they will be mystics. According to some, mystics are people who see the divine, and in part this is true. The late Mary Oliver, for instance, perceived the holy in the depths of nature. But, as I mentioned in chapter 3, mystics may also have the sense that God is lovingly aware of us. This is more than being caught in God's omniscient-but-distant gaze. We feel understood and accepted in all our beauty and shabbiness.

We often talk about Jesus as the perfect revelation of God. We can see God's true self in the life, death, and resurrection of Jesus. But it is also true that in Jesus we experience being seen and known. At least initially, this can feel like being exposed. Take, for example, Luke's account of the call of the first disciples (Luke 5:1-11).

Jesus had just closed a teaching session at the shore of Lake Gennesaret. A large crowd had pressed him to water's edge, so Jesus had commandeered a boat in order to teach from the shallows. Once the lesson had ended, Jesus asked the boat's owner, Peter, to push out to deeper water and to cast his nets. Luke doesn't tell us if Peter had listened to Jesus's teaching. Ostensibly, he could have been there simply because he had returned from fishing. We do know that the night's catch had been a complete bust. Peter told Jesus as much when Jesus asked him to lower the nets, but he did as Jesus instructed anyway. The nets snared so many fish that their weight threatened to swamp both Peter's boat and a second craft that had come alongside to take in the enormous haul. At the sight of such a catch, Peter fell to his knees and told Jesus to step away. "I am a sinful man!" Peter said (v. 8).

There are a number of ways to interpret Peter's confession. He might have been overwhelmed by the power implied by the miracle he had just witnessed, or he might have recognized the divine in Jesus and repented of his sins. I don't reject either of these readings, but I ask you to consider adding another one to them: perhaps Peter felt exposed. He had experienced being seen and known to his very depths, and he was understandably shaken by it. Maybe he expected to be shamed for not measuring up or punished for his imperfections. But after the initial shock, Peter felt a powerful attraction. There is nothing so attractive as being loved as a gift—no conditions, no payback expected. This kind of love is an expression of the lover's very being. No wonder Peter followed Jesus. Love itself had drawn him and sent him into the world with a message—the message of love.

Unfortunately, some of us garble the message when we go into the world. Instead of letting love be the message, we share ideas and insist that faith is all about holding these ideas with dogmatic certainty. As it turns out, though, the certainty some of us insist upon actually damages the faith we were sent by Christ to share.

Certainty Can Damage Our Faith

The disciples once made a perfectly reasonable request: "Increase our faith!" (Luke 17:5). They didn't just say this out of the blue, as if they were sitting around talking about the weather or fishing or how lousy Mary Magdalene's matzo ball soup was and then suddenly blurting out, "Hey, could you pass the salt and a little more faith, please?" Jesus had been teaching them some demanding stuff about what a love-shaped life looks like. For instance, you have to confront people when they've gone off the rails, only you have to do it compassionately, being willing to forgive and ready to mend fences, not just once but over and over and over again. That's a tall order. So, they said, "Increase our faith!" My sense is that they meant something like, "Teach us how to do this and give us the gumption to do it."

Then, Jesus offered them a thought-provoking puzzle. He told them, "If you had faith the size of a mustard seed, you could say to this mulberry tree, 'Be uprooted and planted in the sea,' and it would obey you" (Luke 17:6). Stare at this passage as long as you like, but you're not going to find any explicit instructions about how to forgive or any well-defined concepts about God that you have to accept. At this point in their time with Jesus, the disciples would not have been surprised. Frustrated and confused, maybe, but not surprised. They had learned that Jesus's most challenging teachings rarely convey information directly. Instead, his lessons stretch our souls by loosening our grip on what we feel so certain about. That goes especially for our ideas about God.

Jesus recognizes that religious people—and not so religious people, for that matter—often cling to the ideas about God that their parents, teachers, and preachers gave them while they were children or adolescents. As adults, they equate faith with certainty about those ideas and assume that doubt is the enemy of faith. Shockingly, Jesus encourages his disciples to question their ideas about God because Jesus recognizes that none of our ideas will exhaust the infinite depth of the mystery of God. Because faith is a living, growing relationship, we have to allow our encounters with Christ—right in the midst of the unkempt places we actually live—to challenge our ideas about God. Ironically, a tenacious defense of our ideas about God can sometimes get in the way of a genuine, life-changing encounter with Christ. Let's face it, we are finite, and God is infinite. As one of my philosophy students used to put it, we are small, and God is really, really big. Nothing we ever think, imagine, or say about God adequately captures who God is. Besides, God is a who, not a what. Knowing and loving a "who" is always a work in progress. We never get to the bottom of another person, especially a divine one.

Henry David Thoreau once said, "When any real progress is made, we unlearn and learn anew what we thought we knew before."[2] That is to say, we make progress only by unlearning what we thought we knew so that we can relearn it from a new and better perspective. Or, to paraphrase contemporary theologian Peter Enns, faith is not about certainty.[3] If we want to grow in faith, we have to let go of being so sure that we're right. That's what Jesus was getting at in the illustration about the mustard seed. He said that with faith the size of a mustard seed, we will be able to tell a mulberry tree to hike up its roots and plant itself in the sea.

Initially, this may sound as if Jesus was simply scolding them for their puny faith and telling them how much they could accomplish if they only believed with sufficient zeal. But that would be an odd response to their sincere request for help to become better disciples. It's not very, well, Jesus-y. Look more closely at the picture that Jesus paints. In the faith-infused universe, they would be able to order plants around. At the disciples' command, ordinary trees would uproot themselves, march forward on their little plant feet, and start growing out of the deep blue sea. This is nuts. It's just not how things work. And that's precisely the point. The first step in spiritual growth and genuine faith formation is giving up the idea that faith is about what we know.

This is especially crucial for us in the twenty-first century, who inherited Francis Bacon's dictum that knowledge is power. The experimental method of the natural sciences relies on the ability to predict and control. Knowing is about our power to control a world of things. But faith isn't about knowing things at all. It's about trusting a person—a divine person. It's about trusting that God will be faithful to us and will really be God, a God who is love through and through, no matter what.

Since visiting the concentration camp in which my then-fifteen-year-old mother suffered unimaginable terror and brutality, I've been thinking a lot about certainty and uncertainty. I'm certain that I'll fall if I stumble off a ladder and that I'll suffocate without oxygen. But that kind of stuff isn't what makes life worth living. I need to know it in order to survive, but it's not going to get me out of bed in the morning, much less motivate me to turn the other cheek and love my enemy. No, the big questions are more like these:

- Does love really make a difference in this world?
- Will my life have mattered?
- Will suffering, sacrifice, and sorrow be redeemed?
- Does God really know everything about me and still love me?

I'm not certain about any of this. But I trust; I trust enough to go along with Christ as he keeps changing my mind about God. Just as an openness to change is essential to any healthy human relationship, I believe friendship with God requires our willingness to change our minds about God.

Changing Our Minds about God

Have you ever heard of a Gestalt shift? It's a visual switch of perspective. While looking at an unchanging image, we see first one thing and then another. One famous example is the image that can appear to be a duck or a rabbit. Another familiar example of Gestalt shifts is the vase that can also be two faces peering at each other. The lesson we draw from Gestalt shifts is that perception is interpretation. The universe we inhabit constantly bombards us with an infinite variety of colors, sounds, smells, and textures.

Such complexity is more than we can possibly take in all at once. So we filter and sort everything before we even become aware of seeing it. Philosopher William James said that, if we didn't bring some sort of order to this tidal wave of input, we wouldn't have what we know as experience at all. We would be awash in a "blooming, buzzing confusion."[4]

In other words, what we see, we have already interpreted. Our assumptions—the stories we have already accepted about how life works, what we're like, and what people in general are like—shape our perceptions before we even realize it. The phenomenon of the Gestalt shift suggests that higher consciousness involves checking to see if another perspective is available. As new perspectives emerge, the assumptions that have been shaping (and perhaps narrowing) our perceptions begin to surface.

Gestalt shifts are not only perceptual events. We also can change our minds. Most of us have experienced a change of heart about things or people. We've come upon a new way to see our situation. Jesus came to trigger a Gestalt shift that ultimately would change how we see ourselves, our fellow humans, and the entire universe. As Richard Rohr expresses, Jesus came to change our minds about God.[5] At least, I can tell you that Jesus has done that for me.

As a college freshman, I entered an agnostic phase. During spring break that year, three of us spent a week in Daytona. As we were strolling the boardwalk, a woman roughly our age approached us and asked, "Have you accepted Jesus Christ as your Lord and Savior?" Fresh from studying the problem of evil, I asked the young woman how she squared faith in a loving God with the overwhelming amount of human misery. Unfazed, she responded that God does not cause this suffering. That's when I said, "So God is just a spectator, floating above us at a safe, comfortable distance?" To her credit, the woman acknowledged that I had good questions and invited me to her church to keep looking for answers.

Years later, I realized that my assumptions about God were woven together with and distorted by my childhood experiences of my father.

Distant, uninvolved, and self-absorbed, my father would intermittently make it clear that I didn't measure up to his standard of manhood and would point out changes that I should make. He would then ride off into a sunset of his own choosing until next time. My experiences with my father had influenced my perception of God, though I hadn't been aware of it. In time, Jesus presented me a very different perspective of God in an untidy world. In fact, Jesus has done this a number of times, and I suspect he isn't finished with me yet.

Take, for example, the place of the Ten Commandments in our faith life. Some of us may have inherited assumptions about a law-and-order God: God created us and handed us rules to follow. When we follow the rules, we will be rewarded; violating the rules brings punishment. Reading the Ten Commandments from this perspective renders God as stern, judgmental, and apparently more interested in rules than in real people. If we accept this concept of God, our highest spiritual aspiration will be rigorous adherence to the rules for fear of punishment and desire for reward.

Jesus interprets the Ten Commandments very differently. Look, for instance, at the Sermon on the Mount. Among other themes, Jesus draws our attention to the commandment against killing (Matthew 5:21-22). In essence, he says this: "Scripture tells you not to kill. But I'm here to tell you that even when you fail to respect the dignity of another person, you've basically committed murder. The contempt you heap upon others injures their souls. And just as importantly, your actions reveal that you are suffering from a fatal heart ailment, a soul sickness. You do not recognize God's beloved as worthy of your own love."

Jesus loves us enough to show us the coldness of our own hearts. And he's not telling us merely to shape up or risk losing God's love for us. Jesus is God's love in the flesh come to heal our weak hearts. Jesus shows us that God is lover and healer, not a punishing judge. When we see this about Jesus, the Ten Commandments reveal themselves not as rules but as a beautiful vision for human life: the loving God dwelling in our midst. We are glad

119

for one another's good fortune and safe in each other's embrace. Knowing ourselves as loved with infinite abandon, we love each other without fear and without reserve.

When I look at some images that offer a Gestalt shift, I struggle to see more than one perspective. I have to turn my head to one side or step back a few paces. I need something to move me into a new place to see things anew. That's what Jesus has done in my life. Jesus has changed my mind about God. Or, more accurately, Jesus is helping me be open to new and ever deeper encounters with God by loosening my grip on the ideas I have about God, in a continual invitation to a contemplative faith, one that increases my capacity to love and to hope.

10

CONTEMPLATIVE FAITH

I realized it for the first time in my life: there is nothing but mystery in the world, how it hides behind the fabric of our poor, browbeat days, shining brightly, and we don't even know it.

—Sue Monk Kidd, *The Secret Life of Bees*

There was a time when the term "contemplative faith" suggested to me a life of prayer apart from the common, often hectic rhythms of ordinary life. I thought of monasteries, convents, hermitages, and long silent retreats. Living out a contemplative faith, I assumed, meant to seek the face of God by escaping the noisy distractions of this world. I admire this kind of devotional life, and I believe that some men and women are genuinely called to it. While I am not one of them, I do share the deep longing that motivates them. I yearn for an abiding, life-transforming intimacy with the divine. Maybe you can relate. Maybe you and I are already walking a similar path. The expression of faith to which I am drawn consists of looking for God in all the messy places of our day-to-day life and deriving our hope from our experience of God's presence in the midst of all the beautiful, terrible, sublime, and mundane moments of our existence. I now think of myself as a sort of worldly mystic.

A "worldly mystic" might seem like a contradiction in terms. After all, mystics seek union with God through contemplation, and the terms "worldly" and "mystic" would be incongruous if we were thinking of God as abiding in heaven and contemplation as a form of meditation that detaches us from, or elevates us above, this world. In that case, mystical experience and ordinary experience would be very different. Mystics would be peering beyond this world to the next, and the rest of us would just see what is right in front of our noses. But priest and theologian Ronald Rolheiser tells us that contemplation is not separate from ordinary experience. On the contrary, a contemplative life is one that is devoted to being fully present to what offers itself to us in ordinary, everyday experience.

When we understand the contemplative life in this way, we approach the messy places of everyday life with the anticipation that we will encounter God. Rolheiser writes, "When we are fully awake to ordinary experience, it brings with it a certain *contuition* of God."[1] Contuition is simply sensing God in our world as opposed to imagining or thinking about God as beyond this world. We perceive the infinite alongside the finite, the Creator alongside the created. Rolheiser draws on the idea that there is a difference between contuition and intuition. If we intuit God, we are taking a leap beyond what we can perceive and beyond any logical conclusions we might draw from those perceptions. But if we adopt the contemplative posture of contuition, which is a radical openness to experience as we actually live it, then we perceive the divine in the midst of the ordinary.[2] You might say we have our eyes wide open.

Rolheiser writes, "Mysticism is in fact a very ordinary experience, an experience open to all. . . . Mysticism is being touched by God . . . in a way that is inchoate, namely, in a way that goes beyond what we can think, express, pictorially imagine, and even clearly feel. Mystical knowledge is real knowledge. . . . We *know it*, but . . . mystical experience is, by definition, always partly ineffable."[3] God is always present, and yet we tend to be too distracted or self-absorbed to be aware of that presence. Prayer is essential to the contemplative life. Writers and spiritual teachers like Richard Rohr and Thomas Keating offer great wisdom about and insight into the practices that can awaken us to God's presence. Along with prayer, my own contemplative faith draws heavily on a practice of thoughtful reflection. To put it briefly, I spend time looking back on my lived experiences—through eyes and heart shaped by Scripture stories—and ask a basic question: Where was God in that? Rolheiser might suggest that those of us who live out this kind of contemplative faith belong to the philosophical tradition. He writes, "We perceive everything against a divine horizon. . . . [We] affirm that if we perceive reality properly, this perception brings along with it, however inchoately, . . . the sense that ordinary experience is grounded in God."[4] That is to say, upon reflection we can recognize how God has been lovingly, intimately involved in our life all along. As a result, we grow in our ability to discern God's presence with us in the here and now. Our felt awareness of God's presence is the ground of a contemplative faith and the source of the hope that wells up within us. Please do not hear me asserting that this is the only or even the best way to follow Christ. It is the path that I'm on, and maybe this path beckons you, too. I did not choose this contemplative path through exhaustive study. I stumbled upon it, or maybe it chose me, from a young age.

Against the Divine Horizon

I was eleven years old when Neil Armstrong stepped out of the Apollo 11 lunar module onto the moon's surface on July 20, 1969. My mother and I watched Armstrong's "giant leap for mankind" on a black and white TV in a cheap motel room. Mom had spent most of her remaining cash to give us at least one night sleeping in a bed and a chance to see the moon landing. We were homeless, having fled my physically and emotionally abusive father only a few weeks before. When we left, my mother had no job prospects, no savings, and no reliable support network. We carried with us two suitcases full of our belongings. This is the sort of desperate gamble a mother will take when her husband points a gun at her and then puts that same pistol in her son's face. By the time we settled into living with my maternal grandparents, I had started high school and my address had changed seventeen times. My life contained a heavy dose of chaos. It was in the middle of this disarray that the study of philosophy drew me toward contemplative faith.

Plato introduced me to philosophy. Well, actually, it was Ms. Smith, who was one of my religion teachers in high school. Philosophy was an advanced religion elective when I was a junior or senior, and Ms. Smith started the term with Plato. I was hooked immediately, because Plato sought to make sense out of a constantly changing world. My own life experiences had led me to worry that the only constant in life was that there is no reliable constant in life. You're always standing on shifting sand. For me, this was an unbearable thought. In Plato I found someone who not only recognized the flux of everyday life but also had discovered a deep, abiding truth within the turbulence.

I'm not going to tell you what Plato said as if I were teaching the history of philosophy, though I've taught college-level history of philosophy courses. Instead, I'm going to share with you how I began to reflect upon and interpret my ordinary experience as a result of Plato's influence on me. To be honest, reading Plato may not have this same effect on you. I'm not suggesting that you rush out to your local bookstore and grab a copy of Plato's collected works. I'm sharing with you the way that the Spirit led me to contemplative faith in order to clarify what I mean when I use this phrase. I'm doing this because you may recognize something of your own story here, even though your influences may have been poetry, music, Scripture, film, or a wise friend.

Let's begin with the Allegory of the Cave from Plato's work *The Republic*. Imagine a cave where people have lived since birth. Chains bind each person in a fixed position. Unable to turn to the left or to the right, all they can see is shadows passing to and fro on the otherwise blank wall at the back of the cave. They can't even look at each other. Since these prisoners have never seen anything different, they have taken these shadows for reality. But, of course, they are mistaken. Behind the prisoners' backs a fire is burning. Between the fire and the hapless captives stands a stage for puppets. Another group of people—presumably the captors or their henchmen—march figures in the shape of people, animals, and plants across the stage. The fire acts as a kind of projector that casts shadows of these puppets onto the cave wall.

Eventually, someone sets one of these prisoners free and turns her around. Initially dazed by the fire's light, her eyes gradually adjust, and she comes to realize that what she had thought was most real and most important in life was an illusion. She concludes that the puppets must be what is truly real. But then, someone drags her toward the cave's mouth and tosses her out into the bright noonday sunshine. The sun's rays blind and disorient her. Again, her eyes adjust, and now she sees people, animals, and plants. Just as the shadows on the cave's wall had been dim copies of the puppets, so the puppets themselves are just puny replicas of the real things she can see with her own two eyes. Finally, looking to the sky, she sees the sun. In a flash of insight she recognizes that the sun not only makes everything visible, it sustains all of life. Nothing outside the cave could even exist without the sun's light and warmth. Moreover, everything inside the cave depends on the world outside the cave for its existence. The puppets are copies of the originals, just as the shadows are copies of the puppets, and the fire illuminating the puppet show is a dim copy of the sun.

Plato's point is that everything in this unstable, confusing life of ours points beyond itself to something upon which it depends for its very existence, identity, and meaning. Or, as I would put it now, when we learn how to look, we can see everything under a divine horizon. For Plato, the sun stood for the Good, the pure essence of goodness. And it is the perfect, eternal Good that makes all the imperfectly good things of our life possible as they participate or take part in the Good. In fact, that we can call them good at all points back to the very essence of goodness as their source. For centuries Christian thinkers have drawn a connection between what Plato says about the Good and God.

If we have been taught to think that life's ultimate aim is to leave this life behind and get into heaven, we might hear the Allegory of the Cave as an escape narrative. The goal of life is to leave the cave and dwell in the sunshine for the rest of our lives. But this is not Plato's point. He makes this clear when he writes that, after seeing the truth for herself, this former cave dweller returns to life in the cave. The point of life is not to escape the cave but to see how everything in the cave ultimately points back to the sun—to see everything against a divine horizon.

For instance, consider my dog, Gracie. In Plato's terms, Gracie is good. The infinite Good reveals itself to me in Gracie's finite goodness. There is much more to know about the Good than what I can perceive in Gracie. But she provides me a glimpse of Goodness itself.

Plato taught me to look at the world in front of me as the place where the Good—or God—reaches out toward me to be known—or, more accurately, where God reaches out to embrace me and to be embraced by me. Receiving and returning this embrace is the heart of contemplative faith. This embrace is more than a merely intellectual assent. It's an opening of the heart, mind, and soul, an opening of our entire being. There is more to our earthly existence than meets the eye. From the depths of our messy places, someone is reaching out to us—seeking to connect to us, transform us, and guide us in healing the whole creation. That someone is Christ. As Richard Rohr says, the challenge for us is "to recognize and recover the divine image in everything."[5] Our challenge is to see with eyes illumined by what Jesus calls the "Spirit of truth."

Before his trial, torture, and execution, Jesus taught his friends about the Holy Spirit, the living presence of God within them. He told them, "I still have many things to say to you, but you cannot bear them now. When the Spirit of truth comes, he will guide you into all the truth" (John 16:12-13). The Spirit of truth does not download a library of correct answers into our brains. Believing in Jesus does not make us know-it-alls. Instead, we can think of the Spirit of truth in comparison to light. After all, Jesus called himself "the light of the world" (John 8:12). Just as light makes it possible for us to see, the Spirit of truth helps us see our everyday lives—our real world—against the divine horizon. The Spirit of truth is the light of love, which, as we've seen throughout our journey together, is the beginning of hope.

The light of love leads us to more than a tranquil acceptance or passive, aesthetic appreciation of things as they are. Really seeing the messiness of this world leaves a mark and propels us to action. We begin to see the people we've made invisible, shoved to the margins, and exploited. We begin to see how the world has erased or debased tender, precious dimensions of our own souls. And we begin to see that—even though doing something about all of this will be hard and costly—doing nothing is not an option. That's what it means to take up our cross and follow Jesus. That's what it means to live with hope.

Understandably, we may feel some resistance to this divinely illumined seeing. In her powerful book *Native*, Kaitlin Curtice asks her readers, "How much do we want to see? Because once we see, we cannot un-see. Once we know, we cannot un-know."[6] What Curtice understands, and what we all really know in our gut, is that what we don't see really can and does hurt us. The truth may bring us pain. But only the truth will set us free, and the truth will help us dare to hope even in the messiest of places.

Daring to Hope

Some mornings I wake from a dream so winsome and vivid that I long to lay my head back on the pillow to recapture it, if only for just a moment. Yet, within an hour of rising from bed, the people, landscapes, and improbable adventures of those dreams have mostly faded like the morning mist. I'm left only with the lingering emotions evoked by my nighttime fantasies. It's common to forget our dreams. Researchers insist that everyone dreams, even though just a relatively small percentage of us report that we remember ever having done so.

It occurs to me that from time to time some of us (maybe all of us) need to be encouraged to remember how to dream. By "dream" I don't mean how the brain automatically processes our past while we sleep. What the unconscious mind does with those nightly images, emotions, and memories is crucial for our mental health. But that work is mostly about weaving yesterday into a coherent whole, making sense of what has happened in our lives so far. We also dream about tomorrow. In waking life, our imagination casts visions about how things might be in the future. Yet when we are driven by fear, cynicism, selfishness, or simple weariness, we can forget how to dream. More accurately, we can succumb to or even actively pursue dreams that diminish us and impoverish the world we inhabit. Recapturing and restoring our ability to dream is crucial, because these dreams will dare us to hope, guide our actions, and, as a result, shape the world we will pass on to generations to come.

Dread, unfortunately, is another form of dreaming. We imagine impending doom, heartbreak, and suffering with such intensity and frequency that we assume a habitually defensive posture and strike out repeatedly at perceived threats. Some dreams are narrowly focused on self-interest. We drive relentlessly toward the objects of our own perceived self-interest, justifying harm done to others along the way as collateral damage. These are unhealthy, unholy ways to dream.

In the stories of Jesus's birth and early childhood, Matthew's Gospel teaches us a better way to dream, a way more suitable to our very being as the image of God. Dreaming God's dream and letting it guide our actions fuels our hope as we participate in the coming of the kingdom of heaven on earth. Here's what Matthew tells us:

- When Mary became pregnant, a dream led Joseph to stand by her and to care for her baby (Matthew 1:18-25).
- As Herod descended upon Bethlehem to slaughter every child two years old and under, a dream alerted Joseph to scoop up Mary and Jesus and to flee to Egypt (Matthew 2:13-15).

- Finally, in Egypt, another round of dreams assured Joseph that it was safe to return to Israel and to raise Jesus in Nazareth (Matthew 2:19-21).

These were not merely dreams churned out by Joseph's unconscious. They were God's dreams unfolding themselves in Joseph's own soul. Joseph did not see a perfectly clear vision of the final peace that passes all understanding. Instead, he got word about taking the next step, a limited step that moved in the direction of the world that God dreams.

Joseph was not naive or fanciful. He would have been all too aware of the nightmare the world could be. He had barely escaped the atrocities perpetrated by Herod in Bethlehem. The Roman occupation of Israel was brutal. People he knew and loved had probably been intimidated, beaten, and perhaps even imprisoned or executed by the empire's forces. And yet, he had the courage to dream God's dream, to pursue in his small way the vision that God has for us all. He dared to hope. His charge would be to care for Mary and Jesus, yet his courage arose from a broader vision of God's dream for us all.

God's dream is that we all recognize one another as God's beloved children. No hunger goes unfed. No one wants for shelter or health care. No wars. No crime. Mutual affection displaces loneliness, and love drives out fear once and for all.

When Jesus had grown to adulthood, someone once asked him to name the greatest commandment of all. Jesus responded that we are to love God with every particle of our being and to love our neighbor as if our own life depends upon it. In other words, Jesus taught us to love what God loves, how God loves it. In our fractured, heartrending, messy world, loving like this means that we must remember to dream what God dreams, to dream of a world in which everyone is devoted to making everyone's life worth living.

As it turns out, becoming this kind of dreamer—someone who dares to hope—takes time and patience. Most of all, with ourselves.

Being Patient with Ourselves

In the early '80s I was still a grad student and teaching my very first introductory philosophy course. Some class sessions went well. Others were pretty rocky. On one particular morning, my lecture had induced mass catatonia among my students. I spent the rest of the day kicking myself and muttering, "Stupid, stupid, stupid!" to myself. Later in the afternoon, I strolled up a sidewalk to a nearby watering hole to meet some friends for a whining session. A tow-headed little boy of about nine or ten walked toward me. When we were within ten feet of each other, he caught my eye, smiled, tossed up his hands in a silly-me gesture, and laughingly said, "Stupid Jacob!" How on earth did this kid know my name? Not to mention, how did he know that I'd been calling myself "stupid" for hours? And most incredibly, how did he know just the way to tell me to give myself a break—to show myself a little compassion as a rookie teacher?

I joined my friends and hurriedly told them the story. Our waitress came to the table to take our order. Just then, that little boy strolled up to her. She said, "This is my son, Jacob." He grinned and held up his school bag like a trophy, saying, "I forgot to bring this in. I've got to do my homework." Well, that explained the name thing. But honestly, I think the lesson was a God message: be patient with yourself. As I've come to see, being patient with myself makes it possible for me to be patient with others, and perhaps most important, patience is how we come to know God.

In his letter to the very early church, James writes, "Be patient,... beloved, until the coming of the Lord" (James 5:7). We might hear James saying something like this: "Wait. Hold your temper and tamp down your frustrations. Jesus is coming back. He's going to fix this mess." Many of us think of patience as the struggle to fend off irritability and temper tantrums when we're frustrated or disappointed by delayed gratification or lack of closure. We rush around looking for the pill, food, job, haircut, car, or sex partner who will relieve us, satisfy us, or anesthetize us. Patience is simply waiting to get the thing we don't have. None of us chooses to spend time in the waiting room if we don't have to.

What if we begin to think about patience as the way to acknowledge and to respond to a basic state of our humanity? What if we are restless because God made us that way? As I mentioned in chapter 3, Augustine sees our restlessness as essential to our spiritual life. God created us in order to be in seamless, continuous relationship with us. We are our truest selves in perfect union with our Maker, but in this life our connection with God is always fleeting and incomplete. This means we will be restless. And yet that very restlessness, our deep longing, points beyond this moment to the eternal. Patience is learning to stay with ourselves as imperfect and incomplete beings, learning to be compassionate with ourselves. From that patience with ourselves emerges our ability to be patient with others. Patience is how we love ourselves, how we love others, and how we love God. Richard Rohr writes, "Our task is simply to embody heaven now. We cannot 'get there'; we can only 'be there'—which ironically is to 'be here!'"[7]

Patience is the habitual posture of a contemplative faith. We seek to be right here—with ourselves and with others—as we actually are, because that is where God is. We feel hope because we encounter God in the messy places of this life.

Finding Hope in Messy Places

At the beginning of our journey together, I said that hope is what keeps us going when our hearts are broken, our pockets are empty, and our shoulders sag with heavy burdens. Even if we're lying flat on our face, watching our world unravel around us, or enduring unspeakable cruelty, hope sustains us. It's the feeling in our gut that motivates us to persevere through adversity, resist injustice, and overcome setbacks. My premise has been all along that hope arises from our awareness that God loves us and is always with us, whether we are up or down, on a roll or on the ropes.

When I say that God is with us, I mean that God reaches out to us and embraces us in and through all the circumstances of our life. God created each thing in this vast universe so that God could be in intimate relationship with it, not standing at a commanding distance. That includes you and me. Many of us have felt God's presence in a harvest moon, a setting sun, or a snow-capped mountain range. Nature's beauty and grandeur can fill us with awe. But we know that the world is not all glittering stars and bright rainbows. Misery, terror, want, and oppression mar the planet. Yet, still we can find hope because God shows up even in the ICU and the concentration camp. God dwells with us in beautiful and messy places alike.

Having hope involves discerning a purpose in life. We can endure almost anything as long as we have a "why," a reason for carrying on, that makes the suffering, sacrifice, weariness, or tedium worth it. We derive hope from having the sense that we are answering a call in service to which we will be able to undergo trials, face hardships, and carry heavy burdens. God issues that call to each of us. I am not suggesting that God selects a profession, career, or cause for each and every one of us. God's call to each of us is to become fully human. The Bible tells us that we are created in the image of God and that God is love. So, in whatever we do for a living, our purpose in life is to love what God loves, how God loves it. For the most part, we don't do this with headline-grabbing gestures or history-changing actions. We love at the micro level instead of the macro level.

Whether we are searching for a vaccine or making sandwiches in a deli, doing brain surgery or repairing cars, we can seek to make the world a better place for the people right in front of us. When we're driving carpool, sitting at a desk, mowing the lawn, or paying a cashier, we are being our true selves by simply respecting the dignity and being mindful of the fragility of the people we encounter. This is what habitual love looks like, and these habits are the steady source of hope in our daily lives. Those small acts of love are not really small at all. Our compassion, kindness, patience, and generosity are instances of the divine love welling up within us and pouring out from us for the nurture and healing of the world. They connect us to God and to an ever-widening, ever more diverse circle of people.

Our hope grows as we experience ourselves as belonging to something greater than ourselves: to the God who loves us and, as a result, to the community of God's beloved children. We find hope in our awareness of and reliance upon God's love for us in the messy places of the life we actually live. You, dear reader, are God's beloved. Your life is worth living. God brought you into existence because the creation—because all the rest of us—would be incomplete without you.

Discussion and Reflection Guide

Written by Mike Poteet

This chapter-by-chapter guide offers a structured—though by no means exhaustive—approach for engaging many of the major topics and themes in *Looking for God in Messy Places*, whether as part of a small group or in a time of private reflection.

The guide offers five to eight substantial questions per chapter, some of which integrate scripture passages from the book, to guide group discussion or personal reflection. Though there is no "one right way" to use this resource, here are a few suggestions:

Group Use

- Ensure each participant has a copy of the book.
- Pace yourself, planning to discuss only one chapter per meeting for deeper and richer engagement, or two chapters per meeting for a condensed group experience. (When covering two chapters per meeting, it is recommended you limit yourself to three to four questions per chapter.)
- Before the session, select the questions you feel will be of most interest to your group (or perhaps most challenging to participants, depending upon the group).
- Consider sharing the questions with group members prior to the session so they can reflect and come prepared for discussion.
- Open and/or close the group session with prayer.

- Precede discussion with a simple "Icebreaker" activity, inviting each group member to share one way he or she has been aware of God's presence today or this week.

Individual Use

- Journal about some or all of each chapter's questions as you read, or if you prefer, journal after you've read the whole book.
- Choose one question per chapter that most resonates with or challenges you, and discuss it with a friend.
- Meditate on and pray with the scriptures that are highlighted, either prior to your time of reflection or in a daily prayer period.
- Identify one invitation you sense God extending to you after reflecting on each chapter. Write these down and/or journal about each one.

However you use this guide, may it help you connect with the book's content in deeper ways so that you may ultimately experience a richer relationship with God, who draws close to us to give us hope.

(Note: Excerpts from the book *Looking for God in Messy Places* appear within quotation marks. Passages from the Bible are **boldface** for easy reference during a group session.)

Chapter 1: A Life Worth Living

1. "God doesn't seem to be in the business of fulfilling anybody's actual wish list. Nevertheless, sometimes we can approach God as if this is precisely how God operates—at least for those who *really* believe." Would you agree that this approach to God is "wishful thinking"? Can you remember a situation in which you've approached God with a "wish list"? What happened? How, if at all, would you approach this situation differently now?

2. In contrast to wishful thinking, hope is "a visceral confidence that life is worth living" that "gives us the power to persevere and the stamina to endure." How do you respond to this definition of hope? How closely does it capture what you mean when you talk and think about hope?

3. We're invited to consider the possibility that "some things are not part of God's plan" and "the idea that we live in a cosmos where sometimes things just happen." To what extent do you believe God has "explicit input" into everything that happens in your life, in others' lives, and in the world? In what practical ways do your beliefs about God's will and what happens to and around you shape how you live?

4. How do the suicides of Anthony Bourdain and Tara Condell show "that living is more than surviving"? Have you known people who have died by suicide? Who has helped you respond to their deaths, and how? Did their deaths leave you with questions about life and reasons to live, and if so, what are they?

5. "We are hardwired to yearn for a reason to live." What are your "whys"—your reasons to live? How do you rank them? How, if at all, have they shifted or changed over time?

6. "Even if we believe in life after this life, the anticipation of a better hereafter is not what gives us real hope in the here and now." Do you agree? Why or why not?

7. Read **John 17:1-11**, a portion of Jesus's prayer for his disciples at the last meal they shared before his death.

> **After Jesus had spoken these words, he looked up to heaven and said, "Father, the hour has come; glorify your Son so that the Son may glorify you, since you have given him authority over all people, to give eternal life to all whom you have given him. And this is eternal life, that they may know you, the only true God, and Jesus Christ whom you have sent. I glorified you on earth by finishing the work that you gave me to do. So now, Father, glorify me in your own presence with the glory that I had in your presence before the world existed.**
>
> **"I have made your name known to those whom you gave me from the world. They were yours, and you gave them to me, and they have kept your word. Now they know that everything you have given me is from you; for the words that you gave to me I have given to them, and they have received them and know in truth that I came from you; and they have believed that you sent me. I am asking on their behalf; I am not asking on behalf of the world, but on behalf of those whom you gave me, because they are yours. All mine are yours, and yours are mine; and I have been glorified in them. And now I am no longer in the world, but they are in the world, and I am coming to you. Holy Father, protect them in your name that you have given me, so that they may be one, as we are one."**

How does Jesus define "eternal life" in his prayer? What is the relationship of eternal life to life in "the world"? What is its connection to doing the work God gives? How might it bring hope to Jesus's disciples—in their day and in our own?

Chapter 2: The Power of Love

1. How, if ever, have you wrestled with "the problem of suffering"—
   the tension between God's power and goodness on the one hand,
   and "the cruel realities of this world" on the other? Did you reach
   any insights or conclusions you found helpful?

2. "Jesus bluntly tells us that the universe deals each of us an
   apparently random hand." Read **Matthew 5:43-48**:

   > **"You have heard that it was said, 'You shall love your
   > neighbor and hate your enemy.' But I say to you, Love your
   > enemies and pray for those who persecute you, so that you
   > may be children of your Father in heaven; for he makes
   > his sun rise on the evil and on the good, and sends rain
   > on the righteous and on the unrighteous. For if you love
   > those who love you, what reward do you have? Do not even
   > the tax collectors do the same? And if you greet only your
   > brothers and sisters, what more are you doing than others?
   > Do not even the Gentiles do the same? Be perfect, there-
   > fore, as your heavenly Father is perfect."**

   Does Jesus's talk of how God sends sunlight and rain to everyone
   convince you he believed we live in a random universe? Why or
   why not? How might **Luke 13:1-5** and **John 9:1-3** add to this
   discussion?

3. The author says reflecting on the problem of suffering "can be
   fruitful" but finds love a more fruitful response to suffering. Do you
   agree? Why or why not? How does Jesus's teaching about love for
   enemies empower us for the "imperfect gift" of life?

LOOKING FOR GOD IN MESSY PLACES

4. Read **Luke 9:57-62**:

> **As they were going along the road, someone said to him, "I will follow you wherever you go." And Jesus said to him, "Foxes have holes, and birds of the air have nests; but the Son of Man has nowhere to lay his head." To another he said, "Follow me." But he said, "Lord, first let me go and bury my father." But Jesus said to him, "Let the dead bury their own dead; but as for you, go and proclaim the kingdom of God." Another said, "I will follow you, Lord; but let me first say farewell to those at my home." Jesus said to him, "No one who puts a hand to the plow and looks back is fit for the kingdom of God."**

How is Jesus challenging each of these potential followers to answer the question, "On what am I staking my life?" When have you or someone you know confronted this question? How can we tell whether the "'why' of [our] lives . . . will sustain [us] in even [our] darkest hour"?

5. The author suggests the biblical story of "the Fall"—Adam and Eve's disobedience, told in **Genesis 3**—is a story about "the idea that we are free to make choices in a world shattered in ways not of our own making." What do you think about reading the story in this way? What new, practical possibilities for living might open for us by hearing the story as a story about us more than about "primordial parents who made lousy choices"?

6. "This is why God sent Jesus to live in our midst: to show us how to love with abandon, setting us on the path to remaking this world with God's own power—with love." When, where, and how have you seen love's power to remake the world, in big or small ways?

7. "The greatest challenge to living the way of love is time." What does this mean? Do you agree? Why or why not?

8. In **Luke 20:37-38**, Jesus teaches that God's love "is the power that sustains life beyond the grave." The author calls receiving and sharing that life-sustaining love before we die "a resurrection-shaped life." Where do you see the shape of the resurrection in your own life? What about in the lives of those around you?

Chapter 3: God with Us

1. The author calls the exclamation "wow" "the universal prayer of the wonderstruck." What experiences in your life have left or still leave you wonderstruck? Do you believe God "addresses you with love" in these experiences? Why or why not?

2. In this chapter we explore the theological concepts of God's *immanence* (God's nearness to the created world) and God's *transcendence* (God's distance and independence from the created world). What Bible stories or passages can you think of or locate that depict or describe these divine attributes? How can emphasizing one attribute or the other leave us with a distorted or deficient idea of God?

3. The author suggests God's relationship to the creation is more like that of an artist to the artistic work than it is like that of a watchmaker to a watch. To what would you compare God's relationship to the world, and why?

4. Read **Colossians 1:15-20**, in which the apostle Paul (or an early Christian teacher writing in Paul's name) praises Christ:

> **He is the image of the invisible God, the firstborn of all creation; for in him all things in heaven and on earth were created, things visible and invisible, whether thrones or dominions or rulers or powers—all things have been created through him and for him. He himself is before all things, and in him all things hold together. He is the head of the body, the church; he is the beginning, the firstborn from the dead, so that he might come to have first place in everything. For in him all the fullness of God was pleased to dwell, and through him God was pleased to reconcile to himself all things, whether on earth or in heaven, by making peace through the blood of his cross.**

What does this scripture tell us about God's immanence and transcendence as revealed in Jesus Christ? Does its presentation of Christ evoke awe, confusion, or some other reaction for you? Why?

5. The author suggests that Jesus's resurrection means the risen Christ dwells in everyone and everything: "Finding the risen Christ in our surroundings is our vocation as people of the Resurrection. It's like learning to color outside the lines." When have you unexpectedly met the risen Christ in the people or places around you? How do you know?

6. Of the first Easter, the author writes, "Mary was looking right at the risen Christ, and yet she saw nobody. . . . The good news is that everybody is somebody." When have you been mistaken for "nobody"? Who are the "nobodies" you and your community tend to overlook? How will you tell others to look for the risen Christ in the world's "nobodies," as Mary Magdalene told the disciples she had seen the Lord?

Chapter 4: An Inextinguishable Light

1. In this chapter we read the stories of two women who lived in dark and "dreadful circumstances" in which they nevertheless experienced "a life-giving awareness of God's loving presence"—the author's own mother, and Etty Hillesum. Both were prisoners in Nazi camps. Owensby's mother survived; Etty Hillesum did not. What thoughts and feelings do these women's stories stir in you? What details from their stories most impress themselves upon you, and why? What do their stories tell you about the source and nature of hope?

2. To affirm God is with us, the author writes, is to affirm "God is doing more than merely sitting alongside you. God's love is making you into what Paul called a 'new creation.'" If someone were to ask you how God has been with you throughout your life, shaping you into your "true self," when and where would you tell them to look?

3. "The life of faith on this planet includes not only glimpses of the divine but also moments in which God seems to have left the building." Even Jesus experienced such a moment (**Matthew 27:46**). When, if ever, have you felt God was absent from the world? from your own life? How have you dealt or do you deal with such moments? How would you respond to someone who tells you they struggle with feelings of God's absence?

4. Recall the story of the author preaching at the funeral of the man he had sponsored who died by suicide. The funeral sermon was on the phrase from the Apostles' Creed that declares, in its traditional version, Jesus "descended into hell." Owensby writes, "Jesus precedes each of us into our darkest place. Into our hell." How do you respond to this idea? How might it guide us as we respond to people who feel as though they are in their darkest personal hells?

5. The goal of Brother Lawrence, the seventeenth-century monk, was "to make all of life a continuous prayer." How do or how could you offer what you do, day in and day out, as a prayer to God? How does or how might this offering deepen and amplify your relationships with other people?

6. In this chapter we read of Christmas lights in the "shotgun houses" of New Orleans serving as symbols of hope, reminding us that, in Jesus's birth, "God comes to dwell in the midst of our gloom." How do your own and your congregation's celebrations of Christmas affirm God's "inextinguishable light" shining in our darkness (**John 1:5**)? How can and do Christians celebrate the birth of Christ in ways that communicate this message more clearly to our community?

Chapter 5: Hope and Calling

1. Think about the best job—paid or unpaid, full-time or not—
you ever had. What made it satisfying to you? How did that job
influence or shape who you are today? Would you say the job gave
you a sense of purpose? Why or why not?

2. Following his spiritual director's lead, the author draws distinctions
between a job, a vocation or calling, and a purpose. How helpful do
you find these distinctions? Why?

3. Read **John 21:15-17**, from a story about the risen Christ
appearing to his disciples when they had returned to their jobs as
fishermen after the first Easter:

> **When they had finished breakfast, Jesus said to Simon
> Peter, "Simon son of John, do you love me more than
> these?" He said to him, "Yes, Lord; you know that I love
> you." Jesus said to him, "Feed my lambs." A second time
> he said to him, "Simon son of John, do you love me?" He
> said to him, "Yes, Lord; you know that I love you." Jesus
> said to him, "Tend my sheep." He said to him the third
> time, "Simon son of John, do you love me?" Peter felt hurt
> because he said to him the third time, "Do you love me?"
> And he said to him, "Lord, you know everything; you
> know that I love you." Jesus said to him, "Feed my sheep."**

How is this "conversation about vocation" specific to Peter? How
does it apply to all Jesus's followers? Who are Christ's "lambs"
and "sheep"? What specific forms does tending and caring for
them take?

4. "Most of us will live quite ordinary lives in jobs we take to make
ends meet. . . . Devoting ourselves to helping others in our daily
work makes that work, whatever it may be, seem worthwhile."

Do you agree? How would you respond to someone who claims their daily work offers them no opportunities to help others?

5. "Being ready for death is, paradoxically, the key to living a full, rewarding, and joyful life." Why is this true? To what extent have you seen this paradox at work for people you have known who've died?

6. "Letting go is our contribution to the transformation that God offers us" from earthly to eternal life. What specific steps can we take and disciplines can we adopt now to prepare ourselves "for giving our lives back to God" when we die?

Chapter 6: Loving What God Loves

1. "Whether we realize it or not, whether we name it this way or not, something or someone becomes our god.... Even if we make no conscious decision on the matter, our habitual actions, the patterns of our lives reveal what god we are worshiping, to what we are entrusting our very beings." What habits and patterns of your life do you believe show who or what your god is—who or what gives your life meaning? Do you think the people who know you best would agree? What about someone meeting you for the first time? What are some specific steps we can take to see our god-identifying habits and patterns clearly, to know whether or not we need to make changes to them?

2. "The Bible tells us that loving is the defining human activity," but we don't always love correctly. When have you seen others or yourself loving the wrong things, or loving "the right things in the wrong way"? Why does loving the right things in the right way prove so consistently challenging?

3. The author tells a story about a young woman who asked him and his wife, Joy, "How can you Christians love everyone? ... [T]here are billions of people. What do you mean you love them all?" How would you answer this young woman's question?

4. Read **John 2:1-11**, the first story about a miracle of Jesus in John's Gospel:

   > **On the third day there was a wedding in Cana of Galilee, and the mother of Jesus was there. Jesus and his disciples had also been invited to the wedding. When the wine gave out, the mother of Jesus said to him, "They have no wine." And Jesus said to her, "Woman, what concern is that to you and to me? My hour has not yet come." His mother said**

to the servants, "Do whatever he tells you." Now standing there were six stone water jars for the Jewish rites of purification, each holding twenty or thirty gallons. Jesus said to them, "Fill the jars with water." And they filled them up to the brim. He said to them, "Now draw some out, and take it to the chief steward." So they took it. When the steward tasted the water that had become wine, and did not know where it came from (though the servants who had drawn the water knew), the steward called the bridegroom and said to him, "Everyone serves the good wine first, and then the inferior wine after the guests have become drunk. But you have kept the good wine until now." Jesus did this, the first of his signs, in Cana of Galilee, and revealed his glory; and his disciples believed in him.

How is this story "a showing, a revelation, of God as love"? The author points to some phenomena (caterpillars becoming butterflies, a child's growing in the womb) as other examples of God's transforming love, even if we "take [them] for granted or think of [them] as merely natural." Do you agree? What other signs of God's transforming love do you find in the world? How might God "make water into wine through us"? When, if ever, would you say God has done this through you? through your community of faith?

5. The author writes, "It's a gift to have people who will call me back to my true self." Who are the people in your life who do this for you? How do they do it? Who is someone else you call back to their true selves, and how?

6. Read **Luke 15:1-7**:

Now all the tax collectors and sinners were coming near to listen to [Jesus]. And the Pharisees and the scribes were grumbling and saying, "This fellow welcomes sinners and eats with them."

> So he told them this parable: "Which one of you, having a hundred sheep and losing one of them, does not leave the ninety-nine in the wilderness and go after the one that is lost until he finds it? When he has found it, he lays it on his shoulders and rejoices. And when he comes home, he calls together his friends and neighbors, saying to them, 'Rejoice with me, for I have found my sheep that was lost.' Just so, I tell you, there will be more joy in heaven over one sinner who repents than over ninety-nine righteous persons who need no repentance."

How does Jesus's parable paint a surprising picture of God's love? How does it challenge and invite us "to grow in how we love"?

Chapter 7: Being Us and Being Me

1. "Hope rests in part upon a sense of belonging." When was a time in your life you felt a strong sense of belonging? What does belonging look like? sound like? smell like? taste like? feel like? How would you respond to someone who says they have never truly experienced a sense of belonging?

2. "Being part of an authentic 'we' requires each of us to draw boundaries, clarify values, and sometimes push back against the group's common assumptions and norms." When have you found this to be true in your experience? How did the group to which you belonged respond when you pushed back? When, if ever, have you been part of a group against which someone else pushed back? What happened then?

3. Read **1 Corinthians 12:14-27**, part of the apostle Paul's description of the church as what the author calls "a web of relationships . . . an authentic 'we'" from which our true self emerges:

   > Indeed, the body does not consist of one member but of many. If the foot would say, "Because I am not a hand, I do not belong to the body," that would not make it any less a part of the body. And if the ear would say, "Because I am not an eye, I do not belong to the body," that would not make it any less a part of the body. If the whole body were an eye, where would the hearing be? If the whole body were hearing, where would the sense of smell be? But as it is, God arranged the members in the body, each one of them, as he chose. If all were a single member, where would the body be? As it is, there are many members, yet one body. The eye cannot say to the hand, "I have no need of you," nor again the head to the feet, "I have no need of you." On the contrary, the members of the body that seem

to be weaker are indispensable, and those members of the body that we think less honorable we clothe with greater honor, and our less respectable members are treated with greater respect; whereas our more respectable members do not need this. But God has so arranged the body, giving the greater honor to the inferior member, that there may be no dissension within the body, but the members may have the same care for one another. If one member suffers, all suffer together with it; if one member is honored, all rejoice together with it.

Now you are the body of Christ and individually members of it.

How does Paul's metaphor of the church as Christ's body communicate both unity and diversity, individuality and interdependency, within the church? How well or poorly does this image resonate with your own experience of church life? If Paul were seeking to make his point to Christians in your community today, what metaphor might he use, and why?

4. "When it comes to love, there's always room for more." How have important relationships of love in your life expanded to include other people? Some expansions may seem natural or expected, though no less meaningful—for instance, a couple's relationship expanding to include children. When have expansions of your relationships surprised you? How have others expanded their relationships to include you? How did and does that experience of being included affect your sense of self?

5. This chapter suggests that the classical Christian doctrine of God as Trinity—Father, Son, and Holy Spirit—means "the Holy One *is* a community: three persons perpetually and eternally loving each other." If God is a community in God's own being, how does this

truth affect our understanding of what it means to be created in God's image (**Genesis 1:27**)?

6. "Jesus wants us to treat everyone as part of the 'we,' even if we think they'll make a stinking mess of the place." How well would you say your community of faith lives up to Jesus's expectation of his followers? How well does it expand to include other people? Toward whom do you have to "emulate Jesus's behavior before [your] emotions have caught up with him"? Why?

7. Throughout history we have used "bloodline thinking" to "justify the view that some people are better than others." Nazi Germany's Nuremberg Laws and "Negro blood" laws in the US during the twentieth century are examples. What other historical examples can you identify? Where do you see "bloodline thinking" asserting itself in our nation and in the world today? How is your community of faith speaking and acting against it? How are you?

Chapter 8: How Love Makes a Difference

1. Why does the author say his mother's liberation from Mauthausen Concentration Camp was not the "happy ending" it might be in a movie or a novel? What question did his mother forever after ask herself that he believes Christians must ask themselves, too? When have you most recently struggled—or, perhaps, how are you now struggling—to answer that question?

2. Read **Matthew 13:24-30**, Jesus's parable about a farmer whose field contains both wheat and weeds:

> **He put before [his disciples] another parable: "The kingdom of heaven may be compared to someone who sowed good seed in his field; but while everybody was asleep, an enemy came and sowed weeds among the wheat, and then went away. So when the plants came up and bore grain, then the weeds appeared as well. And the slaves of the householder came and said to him, 'Master, did you not sow good seed in your field? Where, then, did these weeds come from?' He answered, 'An enemy has done this.' The slaves said to him, 'Then do you want us to go and gather them?' But he replied, 'No; for in gathering the weeds you would uproot the wheat along with them. Let both of them grow together until the harvest; and at harvest time I will tell the reapers, Collect the weeds first and bind them in bundles to be burned, but gather the wheat into my barn.'"**

How does Jesus's story speak to us about God's will? How satisfying or dissatisfying do you find the story's view of good and bad, and why? The author says this story can mean, "You have to take the bad with the good. But you do not have to resign yourself to the bad." If so, what are we to do as we let "weeds" grow together with "wheat"?

3. "Love is risky, because powerful and often violent forces prefer this world the way it is. They like it just fine, because they are on top." How have you seen the forces "on top" in this world resist the force of love? When, if ever, have you experienced the risk of opposition to love for yourself? What happened?

4. What messages about the nature and power of love does the author find in the story of Lale Sokolov, the "tattooist of Auschwitz"? What messages do you find in this story? To what examples, if any, of God's love made visible when it seems "the forces of selfishness and violence are having the last word" can you point?

5. From our knowledge of first-century customs, it is likely that Mary had a midwife attending her as she gave birth to Jesus. "Though the baby Jesus cannot be born again, the risen Jesus can be—and *yearns* to be—born on this planet every day in you and me. We are God's midwives here on Earth every time we love." When and most recently have you seen people, including yourself, assisting with God's birth into this world?

Chapter 9: Friendship with God

1. How do you define or describe friendship? Who is or has been your truest friend? How do you know? How is this friendship like or unlike your relationship with Jesus Christ?

2. The author argues "authentic faith focuses on being true to a friend," God in Christ. How is this way of thinking about faith like or unlike the way you think about faith? the way your congregation or Christian tradition thinks about faith? What questions about the nature of faith, if any, does it answer or raise for you?

3. Read **Luke 5:1-11**, a story about one of Simon Peter's earliest experiences of Jesus:

> **Once while Jesus was standing beside the lake of Gennesaret, and the crowd was pressing in on him to hear the word of God, he saw two boats there at the shore of the lake; the fishermen had gone out of them and were washing their nets. He got into one of the boats, the one belonging to Simon, and asked him to put out a little way from the shore. Then he sat down and taught the crowds from the boat. When he had finished speaking, he said to Simon, "Put out into the deep water and let down your nets for a catch." Simon answered, "Master, we have worked all night long but have caught nothing. Yet if you say so, I will let down the nets." When they had done this, they caught so many fish that their nets were beginning to break. So they signaled their partners in the other boat to come and help them. And they came and filled both boats, so that they began to sink. But when Simon Peter saw it, he fell down at Jesus' knees, saying, "Go away from me, Lord, for I am a sinful man!" For he and all who were with him were amazed at the catch of fish that they had taken; and**

so also were James and John, sons of Zebedee, who were partners with Simon. Then Jesus said to Simon, "Do not be afraid; from now on you will be catching people." When they had brought their boats to shore, they left everything and followed him.

The author suggests that Simon felt "exposed," and that in any true encounter with holiness, we are "seen at the most granular level" and "understood and accepted in all our beauty and shabbiness." When, if ever, have you felt "exposed" by God in such a way? How did you respond? What does Simon's response to Jesus show us about the nature of faith?

4. "Shockingly, Jesus encourages his disciples to question their ideas about God. . . . [A] tenacious defense of our ideas about God can sometimes get in the way of a genuine, life-changing encounter with Christ." Do you agree with this characterization of Jesus's teachings? Why or why not? When have you found your ideas about God seriously challenged? How did you respond to the challenge? What happened, and what difference, if any, did the experience make?

5. The author recalls how his difficult relationship with his father influenced his early assumptions about God, and how Jesus in time "presented [him] a very different perspective of God in an untidy world." What are some ways your mind has changed about God over time? How have these changes formed your faith as it is today? To what extent, and why, have they changed your everyday life as a follower of Jesus?

Chapter 10: Contemplative Faith

1. Why does the author call himself a "worldly mystic"? Would you consider yourself a "worldly mystic"? Why or why not?

2. Studying philosophy, especially Plato's philosophy, led the author to view all of life "against a divine horizon"—helping him ask of all his experiences, "Where was God in that?" He affirms that other influences, such as "poetry, music, Scripture, film, or a wise friend," can and do lead other people to ask the same question. What influences most help you look for God in your experiences? How? Why?

3. Read **John 16:12-15**, from Jesus's last conversation with his followers before his arrest and crucifixion:

   > **"I still have many things to say to you, but you cannot bear them now. When the Spirit of truth comes, he will guide you into all the truth; for he will not speak on his own, but will speak whatever he hears, and he will declare to you the things that are to come. He will glorify me, because he will take what is mine and declare it to you. All that the Father has is mine. For this reason I said that he will take what is mine and declare it to you."**

   What do Jesus's words tell us about the role of patience in the life of faith? The author comments, "The Spirit of truth does not download a library of correct answers into our brains." What, then, is the truth into which the Spirit leads us? Why does God guide us into truth over time? How does our gradually being guided into truth glorify God?

4. "Really seeing the messiness of this world . . . propels us to action. We begin to see the people we've made invisible, shoved to the margins, and exploited. We begin to see how the world has erased

or debased tender, precious dimensions of our own souls. And we begin to see that—even though doing something about all of this will be hard and costly—doing nothing is not an option." How does seeing the truth of the world's "messiness" spur you into taking faithful action? How do you see the action you take against the horizon of God's love for and presence with you?

5. The author highlights Joseph, Jesus's adoptive father, as someone in Scripture who dreamed God's dreams for people and for the world and allowed those dreams to shape his actions. What other dreams in the Bible can you think of or find out about that led people to cling to God's values and pursue God's priorities—to love what and who God loves, as God loves them? What can we do to dream God's dreams and make them, in even small ways, realities in our waking world?

6. How has reading and reflecting on *Looking for God in Messy Places* shaped the way you think about hope? What are one or two main ideas from the book that you believe will stay with you in the days, weeks, and months ahead? What is at least one practical action you feel moved to take as a result of engaging with this book, and why?

Acknowledgments

People connect with God in ways that suit their temperament and their circumstances. My sense is that there is no one right way. Along with other daily practices, writing heightens my awareness of God in the midst of my own life. God made me to be a writer. That's not to say that God has made me an especially good or profound writer. It's just that I need to write because I yearn for God.

By contrast, Susan Salley and the rest of my friends at Abingdon Press have made me an author. For that—for their constant encouragement, patience, energy, and support—I am immensely grateful. Mike Poteet did a masterful job developing the study guide for this book. I'm very lucky to have a marketing wiz like Elizabeth Pruitt helping me connect with readers. I want especially to thank Sally Sharpe for her keen and insightful editor's work on the manuscript I submitted. The book you are reading owes much to her gifts, care, and perseverance.

My regular readers will recognize that the title of this book is drawn from my blog: "Looking for God in Messy Places." There are too many of them to mention by name, but I love them and want to say how grateful I am that they take the time to look for God along with me. Their questions, comments, and insights on the blog via the website, email, and social media have touched me, made me rethink, and sent me in new, surprising directions. Thank you, thank you, thank you!

My day job is Bishop of the Episcopal Church in Western Louisiana. I am blessed not only to serve Christ alongside the people in this part of my state, but also to work in a Diocese that values the teaching role of their bishop. Their devotion and hunger for spiritual growth call me to continue to be a bishop who spreads the good news of God's love by writing.

Without the wonderful team in the diocesan office, there would be precious little time for me to write. Canon John Bedingfield, Kathy Richey, Holly Davis, Joy Owensby, Daniel Chapman, Katie Chapman, and the Rev. Christie Fleming work together to make the trains run on time, tell the bishop when and where to show up, and love the people of this diocese along with me. They are simply the best. I also owe thanks to my spiritual director, Dennis Campbell. Our talks help me stay focused and keep my spiritual wheels from falling off.

Finally, I am especially grateful to my wife, Joy. Every thought that makes it to the published page has been tossed back and forth with her on our walks and during our breakfast-time chats. Her good sense, honesty, and patience nurture my mind and my soul. She is my most favorite person ever.

NOTES

Epigraphs

Anne Lamott, *Almost Everything: Notes on Hope* (New York: Riverhead Books, 2018), 3.

Thomas Merton, *The Hidden Ground of Love: The Letters of Thomas Merton on Religious Experience and Social Concerns*, ed. William H. Shannon (New York: Farrar, Straus and Giroux, 1985), 294.

Introduction

Epigraph

Marilynne Robinson, *What Are We Doing Here? Essays* (New York: Farrar, Straus and Giroux, 2018), 226.

1. Anne Lamott, *Grace (Eventually): Thoughts on Faith* (New York: Riverhead Books, 2007), 17–18.

2. Christian Wiman, *My Bright Abyss: Meditation of a Modern Believer* (New York: Farrar, Straus and Giroux, 2013), 86.

Part I: How Love Gives Us Hope

Epigraph

Barbara Kingsolver, *Animal Dreams* (New York: HarperCollins, 1990), 299.

Chapter 1: A Life Worth Living

Epigraph

Annie Dillard, *Pilgrim at Tinker Creek* (New York: Harper, 1974), 245.

1. Mark Manson, *Everything Is F*cked: A Book About Hope* (New York: HarperCollins Publishers, 2019), 9–10.

2. Albert Camus, *The Myth of Sisyphus and Other Essays*, trans. Justin O'Brien (New York: Alfred A. Knopf, 1955), 3.

3. Marta Cooper and Jill Petzinger, "World Weariness," *Quartz*, October 18, 2016, https://qz.com/811186/weltschmerz-theres-a-german-word-people-use-in-times-of-despair-and-its-as-apt-today-as-it-was-in-the-19th-century/.

4. Tara Condell's post was entitled "I Hate the Word 'Bye,' But See You Later Maybe?" and originally appeared on her blog, www.taracondell.com. It has now been taken down. However, the content of the post can be found in Neal Baker, "I'm Coming Home, Dad," *The Sun*, last updated February 1, 2019, https://www.thesun.co.uk/news/8328101/nutritionist-tara-condell-found-hanged-new-york/.

5. Kate Bowler, *Everything Happens for a Reason: And Other Lies I've Loved* (New York: Random House, 2018).

6. Kate Bowler, *Blessed: A History of the American Prosperity Gospel* (New York: Oxford University Press, 2013).

Chapter 2: The Power of Love

Epigraph
Erich Fromm, *The Art of Loving*, Fiftieth Anniversary Edition (1956; New York: Harper Perennial, 2006), 117.

1. Tom is a widely respected Sartre scholar. His biography of the father of existentialist philosophy will remain a standard for years. See Thomas R. Flynn, *Sartre: A Philosophical Biography* (Cambridge: Cambridge University Press, 2014).

2. Michael Curry, *The Power of Love: Sermons, Reflections, and Wisdom to Uplift and Inspire* (New York: Avery, 2018), 8.

3. Curry, *The Power of Love*, 11–12.

Part II: The God Who Shows Up

Epigraph
Anne Lamott, *Plan B: Further Thoughts on Faith* (New York: Riverhead Books, 2006), 275.

Chapter 3: God with Us

Epigraph
Roald Dahl, *The Minpins* (New York: Viking, 1991), 48.

1. Anne Lamott, *Help, Thanks, Wow: The Three Essential Prayers* (New York: Riverhead Books, 2012), 71.

2. Augustine, *The Confessions* (1.1.1). See *The Confessions of Saint Augustine*, trans. John K. Ryan (New York: Doubleday, 1960), 1.

3. See Diana Butler Bass, *Grounded: Finding God in the World—A Spiritual Revolution* (New York: HarperCollins, 2015), 4.

4. Meister Eckhart, "Sermon 53," in *Meister Eckhart: The Essential Sermons, Commentaries, Treatises, and Defense*, trans. Edmund Colledge, O.S.A., and Bernard McGinn (Mahwah, NJ: Paulist Press, 1981), 205.

5. Hildegard of Bingen, quoted in *The Divine Works* in the introduction to *Hildegard of Bingen: Selected Writings*, translated with introduction and notes by Mark Atherton (New York: Penguin, 2005), xxxvi.

6. St. John Chrysostom, "Homily 50 on Matthew," New Advent, accessed December 23, 2020, https://www.newadvent.org/fathers/200150.htm.

7. Mary Oliver, "Turtle," in *Devotions: The Selected Poems of Mary Oliver* (New York: Penguin Press, 2017), 333.

8. Frederick Buechner, *Wishful Thinking: A Seeker's ABC* (New York: HarperCollins, 1973), 52–53.

9. Bobby McFerrin, "Don't Worry, Be Happy," track 1 on *Simple Pleasures*, EMI-Manhattan, 1988.

Chapter 4: An Inextinguishable Light

Epigraph

J.R.R. Tolkien, *The Fellowship of the Ring: Being the first part of The Lord of the Rings* (London: HarperCollins Publishers, 2020), 204. First published in Great Britain by George Allen & Unwin, 1954.

1. The following sketch of Etty Hillesum's life and the passages from her writings are drawn from two sources: David Brooks, *The Second Mountain: The Quest for a Moral Life* (New York: Random House, 2019), 75–81, and Richard Rohr, *The Universal Christ: How a Forgotten Reality Can Change Everything We See, Hope For, and Believe* (New York: Convergent, 2019), 81–83. For a more extensive treatment of her life see Patrick Woodhouse, *Etty Hillesum: A Life Transformed* (London & New York: Bloomsbury, 2009).

2. Brooks, *Second Mountain*, 77.

3. Brooks, *Second Mountain*, 78.

4. Brooks, *Second Mountain*, 78.

5. Brooks, *Second Mountain*, 81.

6. Brooks, *Second Mountain*, 81.

7. Brooks, *Second Mountain*, 81.

8. Henri J. Nouwen, "Foreword," in Brother Lawrence, *The Practice of the Presence of God*, trans. John J. Delaney (New York: Doubleday, 1977), 3.

9. Roland A. Arriaga, "The New Orleans Shotgun House," blog by Archi-Dinamica Architects, LLC, August 12, 2011, https://archidius .wordpress.com/2011/08/12/the-new-orleans-shotgun-house/.

Part III: Remember That You Are Called

Epigraph

Annie Dillard, "Living Like Weasels" in *Teaching a Stone to Talk: Expeditions and Encounters* (New York: Harper & Row, 1982; New York: Harper Perennial, 2013), 70. Citations refer to the 2013 edition.

Chapter 5: Hope and Calling

Epigraph

Parker J. Palmer, *Let Your Life Speak: Listening for the Voice of Vocation* (San Francisco, CA: Jossey-Bass, 2000), 10.

1. Lamott, *Plan B*, 65–66.

2. Emily Esfahani Smith, *The Power of Meaning: Finding Fulfillment in a World Obsessed with Happiness* (New York: Broadway Books, 2017), 96.

3. Smith, *Power of Meaning*, 96.

4. *It's a Wonderful Life*, directed by Frank Capra (California: Liberty Films, 1946).

5. Smith, *Power of Meaning*, 96.

Chapter 6: Loving What God Loves

Epigraph

Ronald Heifetz, Alexander Grashow, and Marty Linsky, *The Practice of Adaptive Leadership: Tools and Tactics for Changing Your Organization and the World* (Boston, MA: Harvard Business Press, 2009), 223.

1. Bob Dylan, "Gotta Serve Somebody," track 1 on *Slow Train Coming*, Columbia, 1979.

2. Jake Owensby, *A Resurrection Shaped Life* (Nashville: Abingdon Press, 2018), 28.

3. Peter Scholtes, "They'll Know We Are Christians," F.E.L. Publications, 1966.

4. "Arche, Strong's G746," *Blue Letter Bible*, accessed December 23, 2020, https://www.blueletterbible.org/lang/lexicon/lexicon.cfm?t=kjv&strongs=g746.

Part IV: Making a Difference. Together.

Epigraph
Marianne Williamson, *The Law of Divine Compensation: On Work, Money, and Miracles* (New York: Harper, 2012), 35.

Chapter 7: Being Us and Being Me

Epigraph
John Donne, "Meditation XVII" in *Devotions upon Emergent Occasions* (New York: Vintage Books, 1999), xvii.

1. J. Philip Newell, *Christ of the Celts: The Healing of Creation* (San Francisco, CA: Jossey-Bass, 2008), 85.
2. Brooks, *Second Mountain*, 10.
3. Manson, *Everything Is F*cked*, 30–40.
4. See, for example, Noam Shpancer, "Action Creates Emotion," *Psychology Today*, October 25, 2010, https://www.psychologytoday.com/us/blog/insight-therapy/201010/action-creates-emotion.
5. Frances Frank Marcus, "Louisiana Repeals Black Blood Law," *New York Times*, July 6, 1983, https://www.nytimes.com/1983/07/06/us/louisiana-repeals-black-blood-law.html.

Chapter 8: How Love Makes a Difference

Epigraph
Brian Eno and David Bowie, "Heroes," track 3 on *Heroes*, RCA Records, 1977.

1. "King Quotes on War and Peace" (quotation from "Loving Your Enemies" in *Strength to Love*), The Martin Luther King, Jr. Research and Education Institute, Stanford University, https://kinginstitute.stanford.edu/liberation-curriculum/classroom-resources/king-quotes-war-and-peace.
2. Heather Morris, *The Tattooist of Auschwitz: A Novel* (New York: Harper, 2018). For a discussion of the fictional and the historical stories of Lale and Gita, see Christine Kenneally, "*The Tattooist of Auschwitz* and the History in Historical Fiction," *New York Times*, November 8, 2018,

https://www.nytimes.com/2018/11/08/books/tattooist-of-auschwitz
-heather-morris-facts.html.

3. The Nicene Creed, *The Book of Common Prayer 1979* (New York: Church Publishing Incorporated, 1979), 358.

4. Sarah Bessey, "Why Everything You Know about the Nativity Is Probably Wrong," *Field Notes*, December 12, 2019, https://sarahbessey.substack .com/p/why-everything-you-know-about-the.

Part V: Faith, Hope, and Friendship with God

Epigraph

Richard Rohr, "Utterly Humbled by Mystery," *This I Believe*, NPR, December 18, 2006, https://www.npr.org/templates/story/story.php?storyId= 6631954.

Chapter 9: Friendship with God

Epigraph

Wiman, *My Bright Abyss*, 7.

1. The General Thanksgiving, *Book of Common Prayer*, 101.

2. Henry David Thoreau, *The Heart of Thoreau's Journals*, ed. Odell Shepard (New York: Dover Publications, 1961), 3.

3. See Peter Enns, *The Sin of Certainty: Why God Desires Our Trust More Than Our "Correct" Beliefs* (San Francisco, CA: HarperOne, 2016).

4. William James, *The Principles of Psychology* (Cambridge, MA: Harvard University Press, 1981), 462.

5. Richard Rohr, *Eager to Love: The Alternative Way of Francis of Assisi* (Cincinnati: Franciscan Media, 2014), 187.

Chapter 10: Contemplative Faith

Epigraph

Sue Monk Kidd, *The Secret Life of Bees* (New York: Penguin, 2002), 63.

1. Ronald Rolheiser, *The Shattered Lantern: Rediscovering a Felt Presence of God*, rev. ed. (1995; New York: The Crossroad Publishing Company, 2001), 23.

2. Rolheiser, *Shattered Lantern*, 26, note 9.

3. Rolheiser, *Shattered Lantern*, 80.

4. Rolheiser, *Shattered Lantern*, 139–140.
5. Rohr, *Universal Christ*, 59.
6. Kaitlin B. Curtice, *Native: Identity, Belonging, and Rediscovering God* (Grand Rapids, MI: Brazos Press, 2020), 105.
7. Richard Rohr, "The Search for the Real," Center for Action and Contemplation, December 20, 2017, https://cac.org/the-search-for-the-real-2017-12-20/.